SRA Imagine It!

Benchmark Assessment

Blackline Masters

Doug Fuchs

Lynn Fuchs

Level 4

Mc Graw Hill   SRA

A Division of The *McGraw-Hill* Companies

SRAonline.com

 SRA

Send all inquiries to this address:
SRA/McGraw-Hill
4400 Easton Commons
Columbus, OH 43219-6188

ISBN: 978-0-07-617646-5
MHID: 0-07-617646-0

1 2 3 4 5 6 7 8 9   QPD   13 12 11 10 09 08 07

Table of Contents

Imagine It! Benchmark Assessment

Benchmark Assessment forms the backbone of the *Imagine It!* assessment system. The *Benchmark Assessment* consists of seven evaluations that are administered periodically throughout the school year. The first Benchmark test is administered at the beginning of the year, and subsequent Benchmarks are administered at the end of each unit.

Imagine It! Benchmark Assessment differs from traditional classroom tests in two important ways. First, each Benchmark samples skills from the entire year-long curriculum, rather than sampling skills taught in the most recent unit. Second, all of the Benchmarks within a grade have the same format, sample the same content, and are of equivalent difficulty. Thus, improving scores on the Benchmark Assessments over the course of the year indicate students' increasing mastery of the grade-level curriculum. (For a more detailed explanation of the rationale of the structure of the Benchmark Assessments, see the *Imagine It!* Professional Development Guide to Assessment.)

Components of Benchmark Assessments

The Benchmark Assessments have three major components:

• The 100-Point Skills Battery

• Oral Fluency

• Expository Writing

The 100-Point Skills Battery

This component samples skills from strands within the grade level curriculum. Reading comprehension, vocabulary, grammar, usage and mechanics, and spelling comprise the skills battery in Level 4. Each strand has been assigned a weight in accordance with its importance in the curriculum to reach the total of 100 points. The table below shows the strands in Level 4, the number of items in each strand, the weight given to each item within a strand, and the setting in which the assessment of the strand is administered.

Level 4

Strand	# Items	Total weight	Format	Setting
Comprehension	20	40	Multiple Choice	Group
Vocabulary	10	30	Multiple Choice	Group
Grammar, Usage, and Mechanics	10	20	Multiple Choice	Group
Spelling	10	10	Multiple Choice	Group

Oral Fluency

The Fluency portion of the ***Benchmark Assessment*** is a direct measure of students' reading fluency. It also serves as a general, overall indicator of a student's reading competence. For example, students who score poorly when reading text aloud in a fixed time are the same students who have poor decoding skills, whose ability to recognize words automatically is inadequate, who have limited vocabularies, and who have difficulty understanding what they read.

Passage Reading Fluency

Students will have one minute to read aloud the Oral Fluency passage for each Benchmark test, although they are not expected to complete the passage before the minute has passed. You will time each student, noting any errors the student makes and calculating his or her correct words per minute (WPM) and accuracy rate from the instructions on page x of the introduction. Because this portion of the Benchmark Assessment must be individually administered, you will need to allot at least 2 minutes for each student in your classroom so that each student has time to read to you and so that you have enough time to transition from student to student.

Expository Writing

A Writing assessment is included with the first, fourth, and seventh Benchmark Assessments at this grade level. For each Writing Assessment, make a copy of the prompt and make sure students have paper and writing materials. These prompts for expository writing are similar to the type of prompt found in high-stakes tests. A checklist is provided to help students focus their work. Students will be graded using the Four Point Rubrics for Expository Writing found on page 138.

Students who fall below cutoffs in the writing should be monitored during their classroom writing assignments. If a student's writing shows little or no improvement, do not wait until the next Benchmark to intervene. Provide the necessary support to ensure the student begins writing cohesive text in a grade-level appropriate manner.

Purposes of Benchmark Assessments

The Benchmark Assessments serve three major purposes in the classroom:

• Screening

• Progress Monitoring

• Diagnosis

Screening

Screening is the process of measuring all students in a class to identify the subset of students who, without special attention, are in danger of scoring poorly on the end-of-year high-stakes tests and long-term reading failure. Cutoff scores for the Benchmark Assessments are provided below. At the beginning of the year, and then periodically throughout the year, any student who falls below the cutoff score on the 100-Point Skills Battery, Fluency Assessment, and Expository Writing Assessment should be considered for intervention. That student's progress should be closely monitored through weekly fluency assessments.

100-Point Skills Battery

Benchmark 1	Benchmark 2	Benchmark 3	Benchmark 4	Benchmark 5	Benchmark 6	Benchmark 7
20	30	42	54	66	78	90

Fluency Cutoffs–Oral Reading Fluency

Benchmark 1	Benchmark 2	Benchmark 3	Benchmark 4	Benchmark 5	Benchmark 6	Benchmark 7
68	82	96	110	124	138	152

Expository Writing Cutoffs

Benchmark 1	Benchmark 2	Benchmark 3	Benchmark 4	Benchmark 5	Benchmark 6	Benchmark 7
11	N/A	N/A	13	N/A	N/A	15

Progress Monitoring

Because each of the Benchmark Assessments is constant in difficulty and format, they provide a means for measuring the progress of all students in a classroom over the course of the academic year. Improving total scores on the Benchmark Assessments indicate a student's increasing mastery of the language arts curriculum.

Diagnosis

Because each of the segments of the Benchmark Assessments provide a separate score in each of the strands of the curriculum, they can be used to identify the specific curriculum areas that are strengths or weaknesses for a student or across a classroom.

If students score below the cutoff for any Benchmark Assessment, use one or more of the following options to help students get back on track:

- **Reteach**—use this with students who need extra help with comprehension; spelling; vocabulary; and grammar, usage, and mechanics

- **Intervention**—assign this to students who need more intensive help with comprehension; spelling; vocabulary; grammar, usage, and mechanics; oral fluency; and writing

- **Workshop Planner Activities**—have students work on these activities to improve their comprehension; spelling; vocabulary; oral fluency; and grammar, usage, and mechanics skills

- **Leveled Readers (Approaching Level)**—allow students to read these leveled books to improve their comprehension, vocabulary, and fluency skills
- **Leveled Science Readers (Approaching Level)**—distribute these books for students to read to improve their comprehension, vocabulary, and fluency skills
- **Leveled Social Studies Readers (Approaching Level)**—hand out these books to students to read in order to improve their comprehension, vocabulary, and fluency skills
- **Workshop Kit**—utilize the activities in this kit to give students extra practice with comprehension; vocabulary; grammar, usage, and mechanics; and oral fluency skills

Attributes of Benchmark Assessment

The Benchmark Assessments differ from traditional tests because each Benchmark Assessment tests skills from the entire year-long curriculum; by contrast, many classroom tests address only the skills or content most recently taught. This means that the Benchmark Assessments at the beginning of the year may be very difficult for some students. It is important for both you and your students to understand that the Benchmark Assessments are designed in a way that permits students to show growth (i.e., to improve or obtain increasingly higher scores) over the school year, as you teach them the important skills and strategies incorporated within *Imagine It!* On the 100-Point Skills Battery, for example, students are not expected to answer every question correctly at the beginning of the year. The hope is that by the end of the year, students will answer all questions correctly on the 100-Point Skills Battery. On the Fluency section, a similar situation exists. Students are not expected to complete the entire assessment in the time limit at the beginning or even at the end of the year. The Fluency time limit is deliberately set to reduce the possibility that students will complete the task before time is up.

The Benchmark Assessments provide unique assessment opportunities in the classroom, including the ability to monitor students' progress through the consistency of the tests and the ability to prepare students for high-stakes tests.

Consistency

The Benchmark Assessments are designed to be equivalent in format, content, and difficulty. This equivalency is the key to monitoring a student's progress over the course of the school year. It is equally important for you to maintain consistency as you administer the Benchmark Assessments over the course of the school year. For example, students' performance on tests may vary depending on the time of day or the day of the week. Therefore, it is important to administer each Benchmark Assessment over the course of the year on the same day of the week, at the same time of day, and in the same classroom or space. Also, it is important to follow the time limits for each strand in order to maintain consistency over the course of the school year in the amount of time students have to work on the assessments.

Preparation for High-Stakes Tests

An added benefit to the Benchmark Assessments is that they should help students and teachers prepare for end-of-the-year high stakes tests. Most importantly, the scores on the Benchmark Assessments provide the information you need to identify which students need additional attention on a certain portion of the curriculum. In addition, the Benchmark Assessments may also provide an opportunity for students to practice taking tests in a formal setting. These assessments are similar in format to many high-stakes tests in that they sample a variety of skills, have several component sections, are timed, and have similar question formats. With the administration of each Benchmark Assessment, you have the opportunity to help students practice their test-taking skills for end-of-the-year testing.

On the day before the administration of a Benchmark Assessment, remind students to get a good night's sleep and eat a good breakfast, just as they would before end-of-the-year testing. On the day of the assessment, set up the classroom in the same way as will be done for high-stakes testing by separating desks, using student "offices," and so on. This will help your students become accustomed to this form of test taking.

After students have taken an assessment and you have scored it, you can use it for discussion purposes. Because specific questions are not repeated across Benchmark Assessments, you can use these questions to highlight certain skills or to discuss strategies for attacking a question or general test-taking strategies.

Administration of Benchmark Assessments

Time Limits

Time limits for each 100-Point Battery test are as follows:

Strand	Time Limit
Comprehension	20 minutes
Vocabulary	10 minutes
Grammar, Usage, and Mechanics	10 minutes
Spelling	10 minutes

Test-Taking Procedure

Administer the tests without aiding the students in any academic way. While logistical questions may be answered ("Is this the right page?" or "Do I have a page missing?"), you should not answer questions such as "What is this word?" or "What am I supposed to do?" that may give the student an advantage academically.

Assemble the pages of the group administration part of the Benchmark test that you are giving and make a copy for each student. Staple or clip the pages together for each student, making sure that the sections of the Benchmark are in this order: Comprehension; Vocabulary; Grammar, Usage and Mechanics; and Spelling.

Once you are ready to administer the 100-Point Battery of the Benchmark test, distribute a copy of it to each student. Be sure all students have a copy of the test. Once they do, say:

Please take your pencil and fill in the information at the top of the front page of the booklet. Today's date is on the board. Please write neatly. When you have finished, put down your pencil and wait for my instructions.

Circulate around the room to be sure students fill in this information completely and accurately. Once they have, say:

You will be taking the comprehension *part of the test first. Read all the directions completely as you come to them. You will be given* **20** *minutes to complete this section of the test. I will write '5 minutes' on the board when there are five minutes left. This section of the test will end when you come to a "STOP" sign. When I say "Time," that means this section is over. You should put down your pencil immediately and wait for my directions.*

Ask students if they understand the process. Then say:

As you read and answer the questions, be sure to choose only one answer for each question. Be sure that you fill in the circle for each answer completely. If you erase any marks, make sure that you erase them completely. Do not look ahead or mark anything on any other section except this section.

If you finish before the time is up, you may check your work. Be sure that your answers are clearly marked and that all unwanted marks are erased completely.

If you have questions, you may raise your hand and I will come to your desk. However, I cannot tell you answers, give you hints about answers, or explain test questions.

Do you have any questions now? You may begin.

When time is up for the section, say:

The time is up for the comprehension section. Please put down your pencils.

Continue with the remaining sections of the benchmark test in the same fashion, changing directions in relation to time limit. Add the following directions so that students understand what is expected of them: *When you reach the "STOP" sign, you may look back over your answers in this section. However, you cannot go back and work on sections that have been completed earlier.*

When the Benchmark test is complete, collect all the tests. Allow time for a short break before administering Fluency and/or Writing assessments.

Oral Fluency Assessment

You will find oral fluency assessments for each Benchmark test.

Make a copy for yourself of the Oral Fluency Assessment for each student you will be assessing. Provide students with a copy of the passage. The teacher and student versions follow each other in the ***Benchmark Assessment*** book. Be sure you have a pen or pencil, a stopwatch or other timer, and extra paper to record any observations. Record the student's name, the date of the assessment, and the results of the assessment.

Have the student sit comfortably at a table with you. Seat yourself and the student so that you can mark the assessment unobtrusively without distracting the student.

Say: *Here is a selection I would like you to read aloud for me. I am going to listen to you read and take some notes. The notes I take will help me learn how well you can read. Read the selection carefully and do your best. Are you ready?* (Check to be sure the student is ready.) *You may begin now.*

Start the timer or watch as the student begins to read. You may pronounce any proper nouns with which the student is unfamiliar. Do not count these words as errors. At the end of one minute place a bracket ( ]) at the end of the last word the student reads.

The following guidelines will help you score the assessment accurately and consistently.

- Self-correcting should not be counted as an error.

- Repeating the same mistake should be counted as only one error.

- Hesitating for more than five seconds—at which point you would have provided the word—should count as an error.

- Draw a line through any word that is misread. Count this as an error. If possible, note the type of error. (Misreading *short* a *as short* e, *reading* get *as* jet, and so on).

- Words the student omits should be counted as errors, even if you prompt the student.

- Indicate with a caret extra words that have been inserted. If possible, write the inserted word. Count insertions as errors.

- Draw an arrow between words that have been reversed. Count these as one error.

- Students might repeat words on occasion. Do not count this behavior as an error.

- Complete the Reading Rate and Accuracy box after a student has read for the minute. This will give you the student's correct words read per minute (WPM) and the student' accuracy rate.

- Enter the student's WPM at the top of the page. Then transfer that number to the appropriate Benchmark Assessment Record and note whether the student has reached the expected fluency cutoff.

- Next examine the student's accuracy rate. Reading accuracy should remain constant or gradually increase within a grade and between grades, until it stabilizes at ninety percent or higher. You may find it helpful to compare a student's accuracy rate after each administration to ensure that it remains constant or increases.

- Complete the Reading Fluency scale at the bottom of your Oral Fluency Assessment page. These qualitative measures indicate your subjective judgment of how the student compares with other students who are reading at grade level.

- Note the types of errors a student makes. Track if similar errors occur or are corrected as the student progresses through the Benchmarks.

Time Management

The Benchmark Assessments are administered using a time frame that matches content and time expectations found in high-stakes testing. As such, the expectations placed on your students are both realistic and demanding. In the early Benchmark tests, you will find that students will not finish sections or the entire test on time. If this behavior continues as Benchmark tests progress, use your professional judgment as to whether maintaining consistency of time limits is adversely affecting your students' reaction to the Benchmark Assessment. If you believe this is the case, do allow for some leeway on the time. However, do not add so much time that the data you gather is no longer an accurate representation of student achievement. For example, adding ten minutes to the comprehension will affect your knowledge of whether students can quickly and accurately access and process grade-appropriate text.

Teacher Records

Benchmark Assessment offers a variety of means to mark and note student progress. Initially, you should grade the Benchmark tests section-by-section and list the total score on the first page of the test after the student name. Use the Answer Sheets located on pages 117–137 to assist you. You will find it beneficial to store each student's pages and test booklets in a folder or binder and then transfer that information to the Benchmark Assessment Record and the Benchmark Tracking Chart.

Benchmark Assessment Record

A Benchmark Assessment Record page is provided for each test at the back of this book. The spaces following the student's name allow for the recording of student scores in each assessment strand; the total scores achieved in the 100-Point Skills Battery; fluency scores; writing scores; and whether students have reached the necessary cutoff points.

The Benchmark Assessment Record provides an easy way to record student growth across the year.

Benchmark Tracking Chart

Duplicate this page for each student. The cutoffs for each 100-Point Battery are listed. Map student numbers on this chart using data from the test booklets and/or the Benchmark Assessment Record. Plotting student scores will give you a quick visual appreciation of progress, standing, and student trends. You can create a similar page to chart student's fluency numbers, if you wish.

Name _____ Date _____ Score _____

Comprehension

Read the following story. Then answer questions 1–10 relating to the story. You may look back at the story to find the answers.

"Let's pick some berries," Grandma said to Nick one morning.

Nick followed Grandma down the dirt road to the woods. At the edge of the woods, low bushes and vines grew all tangled together. Nick could see fat, juicy blackberries hanging from thin stems. Grandma warned him to watch out for thorns. She showed him how to pick the berries gently. If you crushed them, they stained your hands deep purple.

Grandma told Nick that long ago, people often used the leaves and the berries to make hair dye. Her own parents dried the berries and used them during the winter.

"They'd crush them to make powder," Grandma said. "Then all winter long, my mother would mix the powder in water. She didn't know it, but she was giving us Vitamin C. We didn't have frozen orange juice back then. You couldn't buy fruit juices in the grocery store all year long."

"Back then," she continued, "we also used to make ink with these berries. First we'd smash the berries through a strainer with a spoon to get rid of the seeds. Then we would add a little vinegar and salt to the juice. Vinegar kept the color dark, and salt kept it from spoiling."

GO ON

Comprehension (continued)

Nick thought it sounded like fun and asked, "Could we do that?"

"Only if you promise to use the ink outside," she said with a laugh. "My mother made me promise that, but I disobeyed her once."

She told Nick the story. One rainy day, Grandma had wanted to write a letter to her best friend. She shouldn't have, but she took the ink upstairs to the bedroom she shared with her sister. When she heard footsteps on the stairs, she looked for some way to hide the bottle. She grabbed a piece of cloth from her sister's bed and draped it over the bottle.

Her older sister came into the room looking for her new white dress. It was then that Grandma realized the cloth over the ink was her sister's dress. She slid the ink under the bed and handed her sister the dress. Her sister screamed. In the middle of the skirt was a purple ring.

They washed the dress, but the stain did not come out. Then Grandma had an idea. She used the jar rim to make purple circles all over the skirt.

"A lot of my sister's friends liked that dress and asked where she bought it," Grandma said. "But it was always our little secret."

Comprehension (continued)

1. This story is mostly about
- Ⓐ how to decorate a plain white dress.
- Ⓑ the best places to find blackberries.
- Ⓒ a grandmother telling a story to a boy.
- Ⓓ how painful it is to be stuck with thorns.

2. Where were the blackberry bushes?
- Ⓐ at the edge of the woods
- Ⓑ in Grandma's back yard
- Ⓒ at the blackberry farm
- Ⓓ in the middle of a field

3. Why were the berries smashed through a strainer?
- Ⓐ to make the ink darker
- Ⓑ to sweeten the juice
- Ⓒ to remove the seeds
- Ⓓ to put in the Vitamin C

4. What sounds like fun to Nick?
- Ⓐ making ink from blackberries
- Ⓑ making juice from a powder
- Ⓒ putting a design on white cloth
- Ⓓ writing a letter to his friend

5. Who was Grandma writing a letter to?
- Ⓐ Nick
- Ⓑ a friend
- Ⓒ her sister
- Ⓓ Nick's mother

Comprehension (continued)

6. Where was Grandma allowed to use her ink?

Ⓐ upstairs

Ⓑ outside

Ⓒ at school

Ⓓ on cloth

7. Why does Grandma's sister scream?

Ⓐ She has caught Grandma disobeying her mother.

Ⓑ She sees that her new white dress has been ruined.

Ⓒ She got stuck with a blackberry thorn.

Ⓓ She is calling to somebody who is outside.

8. In the story, which of these cannot be made from blackberries?

Ⓐ juice

Ⓑ ink

Ⓒ hair dye

Ⓓ a dress

9. From the story, you know that

Ⓐ Nick's mother did not know the dress story.

Ⓑ Grandma's sister is still mad about the ruined dress.

Ⓒ Nick did not believe Grandma's story.

Ⓓ Grandma did not know she had grabbed her sister's dress.

10. A good title for this story would be

Ⓐ "Grandma's Blackberry Stories"

Ⓑ "Nick Writes a Letter"

Ⓒ "Grandma Disobeys Her Mother"

Ⓓ "Our Little Secret"

Name _____ **Date** _____ **Score** _____

Comprehension

Read the following selection. Then answer questions 1–10 relating to the selection. You may look back at the selection to find the answers.

Some people think the Egyptians used thousands of slaves to push the blocks for the pyramids. But one man in Florida claimed to know how they did it. He said one person could move those huge blocks. To prove it, he built a castle out of heavy coral blocks by himself.

Ed Leedskalnin came to America when he was a young man. He had only gone to school until fourth grade. Then he worked in lumber camps. Ed's father was a stonemason, so Ed knew how to cut stone. He also discovered a way to lift heavy things without help.

Ed was only a little over five feet tall. He weighed about one hundred pounds. Working alone, he cut out blocks from a thick bed of coral. Most of the castle walls are eight feet high and four feet wide. The walls weigh more than fifty-eight tons each. Yet he moved all of the coral blocks into place alone.

It took him twenty-eight years to finish the whole building. Before he put up the walls, he made many huge carvings inside. One is a table in the shape of a heart that weighs five thousand pounds. Ed cut a hole in the center of the table. Inside it, he placed a plant that grows up through the hole. That plant has been there for more than fifty years now.

GO ON

Comprehension (continued)

Many other carvings adorn the castle. Ed put a huge stone rocking chair at the top of a large block of coral. The chair weighs three tons. He lifted it up there by himself. He also made a moon fountain. There was a fishpond in the middle. The quarter moons on each side weigh eighteen tons. He lifted them into place alone.

How did he do all this without help? Even engineers are not sure. Ed said it was easy if you knew the secret. However, he never gave up his secret. He may have used levers and rollers. These are tools that let a person move heavy objects. Some people think Ed used magnets of some kind. Ed once said that all matter could be moved by magnetism at least a little bit. They think he figured out how to use magnetic force to move the blocks. It is too bad he did not share his secrets. He died in 1953. Now no one will ever know how he built his coral castle, unless they can figure it out like he did.

Comprehension (continued)

1. This selection is mostly about

   Ⓐ how the ancient Egyptians built their huge pyramids.

   Ⓑ how one man can lift very heavy things without help.

   Ⓒ how to carve fancy designs into large pieces of coral.

   Ⓓ how one man proved he knew the Egyptians' secret.

2. How long did Ed Leedskalnin go to school?

   Ⓐ until high school

   Ⓑ until fourth grade

   Ⓒ through college

   Ⓓ through sixth grade

3. Which of these best describes Ed Leedskalnin?

   Ⓐ an engineer with a lot of experience

   Ⓑ an immigrant with little education

   Ⓒ a scientist who studied the pyramids

   Ⓓ a dreamer who wanted to go to Egypt

4. Ed probably learned about cutting stone from

   Ⓐ his neighbor.

   Ⓑ an engineer.

   Ⓒ his father.

   Ⓓ a family friend.

5. Why did the castle take so long to finish?

   Ⓐ Ed did all of the work by himself.

   Ⓑ Ed had to find lots of coral.

   Ⓒ Ed had to figure out how to cut the coral.

   Ⓓ Ed had to find other people to help.

GO ON

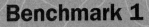
Comprehension (continued)

6. What did Ed do before he put up the castle walls?

    Ⓐ He learned how to build a magnet.

    Ⓑ He studied the pyramids of Egypt.

    Ⓒ He discussed the job with some engineers.

    Ⓓ He made many carvings inside.

7. What is in the center of the moon fountain?

    Ⓐ a magnet

    Ⓑ a pond

    Ⓒ a moon

    Ⓓ a chair

8. Why do some people think Ed used magnetic force to move the rocks?

    Ⓐ He said something about matter being affected by magnetism.

    Ⓑ All of the other possible explanations do not make as much sense.

    Ⓒ Engineers have found magnets under the base of the castle.

    Ⓓ He told his wife he was going to use magnets.

9. Which of these did Ed probably not use?

    Ⓐ cranes   Ⓒ rollers

    Ⓑ levers   Ⓓ magnets

10. From the selection, you know that

    Ⓐ Ed was a very large and strong man.

    Ⓑ the Egyptians used ramps to move rocks.

    Ⓒ nobody has quite figured out how Ed moved the coral.

    Ⓓ Ed did not know how to make carvings out of rock.

Vocabulary

Read each item. Fill in the bubble for the answer you think is correct.

1. <u>Repay</u> means
   - Ⓐ pay too late.
   - Ⓑ not pay.
   - Ⓒ pay back.
   - Ⓓ pay too much.

2. <u>Clear</u> is the base word in <u>unclear</u>. <u>Unclear</u> means
   - Ⓐ without any friends.
   - Ⓑ hard to understand.
   - Ⓒ almost empty.
   - Ⓓ not on time.

3. <u>Geology</u> means
   - Ⓐ the study of farming.
   - Ⓑ the study of weather.
   - Ⓒ the study of books.
   - Ⓓ the study of the Earth.

4. What word means about the same as <u>odd</u>?
   - Ⓐ usual
   - Ⓑ dim
   - Ⓒ strange
   - Ⓓ awake

5. What word means about the same as <u>crouched</u>?
   - Ⓐ stood
   - Ⓑ ran
   - Ⓒ cried
   - Ⓓ bent

Vocabulary (continued)

6. What word means the opposite of <u>possible</u>?

    Ⓐ likely   Ⓒ predicted

    Ⓑ certain   Ⓓ heavy

7. Which word BEST completes both sentences?

    The ___ is in the drawer.

    You will need a ___ to sharpen that.

    Ⓐ paper   Ⓒ tool

    Ⓑ knife   Ⓓ file

8. Which word BEST completes both sentences?

    I came in ___ in the race.

    The light came on for about a ___.

    Ⓐ last   Ⓒ second

    Ⓑ minute   Ⓓ third

9. The big bed was <u>cozy</u> on a cold night. <u>Cozy</u> means

    Ⓐ hard.   Ⓒ cold.

    Ⓑ warm.   Ⓓ large.

10. Do not <u>misplace</u> your book or you will waste time looking for it. <u>Misplace</u> means

    Ⓐ carry.   Ⓒ read.

    Ⓑ find.   Ⓓ lose.

Grammar, Usage, and Mechanics

Read each question. Fill in the bubble beside the answer in each group that is correct. If none of the answers is correct, choose the last answer, "none of the above."

1. Which sentence is written correctly?

Ⓐ Elizabeth is the name of the queen of england.

Ⓑ Elizabeth is the name of the Queen of England.

Ⓒ Elizabeth is the name of the queen of England.

Ⓓ none of the above

2. Which sentence is written <u>incorrectly</u>?

Ⓐ Balls, bats, and gloves are used to play baseball.

Ⓑ I had a sandwich, soup, and milk for lunch.

Ⓒ Stephen likes apples, bananas and oranges.

Ⓓ none of the above

3. Which sentence is written correctly?

Ⓐ Rob's favorite song is The Way We Were.

Ⓑ Rob's favorite song is "The Way We Were."

Ⓒ Rob's favorite song is, "The Way We Were."

Ⓓ none of the above

4. Which sentence is written <u>incorrectly</u>?

Ⓐ "It is beautiful!" Jose said.

Ⓑ "It's the end of the world the actor said."

Ⓒ Gerrald whispered, "I need some water."

Ⓓ none of the above

5. Which sentence is written correctly?

Ⓐ The horse ran around more happiest in the snow.

Ⓑ The horse ran around more happier in the snow.

Ⓒ The horse ran around most happy in the snow.

Ⓓ none of the above

GO ON

Grammar, Usage, and Mechanics (continued)

6. Which sentence is written <u>incorrectly</u>?

   Ⓐ Carl and Kwame runs to the store.

   Ⓑ She travels to Europe and Africa.

   Ⓒ Pizza and cookies are my favorite foods.

   Ⓓ none of the above

7. Which sentence is written correctly?

   Ⓐ I am going to buy me a fan.

   Ⓑ I am going to buy myself a fan.

   Ⓒ I am going to buy mine a fan.

   Ⓓ none of the above

8. Which sentence is written correctly?

   Ⓐ No one knew what to expect after the change is made.

   Ⓑ No one knew what to expect after the change was made.

   Ⓒ No one knows what to expect after the change will be made.

   Ⓓ none of the above

9. Which sentence contains a compound predicate?

   Ⓐ The tree growing in the pot is pretty.

   Ⓑ A truck slowed down and turned into the parking lot.

   Ⓒ The door to the basement has a broken lock.

   Ⓓ none of the above

10. Which sentence contains a dependent clause?

   Ⓐ I know what I am doing.

   Ⓑ The customer asked for help from the clerk.

   Ⓒ She left her jacket here, and Dan came back to get it.

   Ⓓ none of the above

Spelling

Read each group of words. Only one of the words is spelled correctly. Fill in the bubble under the word that is spelled correctly.

1. proven   provne   porven   provin
    Ⓐ   Ⓑ   Ⓒ   Ⓓ

2. bicicle   bicycle   bycicle   bisicle
    Ⓐ   Ⓑ   Ⓒ   Ⓓ

3. ratf   reft   rafte   raft
    Ⓐ   Ⓑ   Ⓒ   Ⓓ

4. laeder   leadre   leader   leeder
    Ⓐ   Ⓑ   Ⓒ   Ⓓ

5. fairle   fairly   fiarly   frialy
    Ⓐ   Ⓑ   Ⓒ   Ⓓ

Spelling (continued)

In each sentence, look for the underlined word that is spelled incorrectly. Focus on just the underlined word. Fill in the bubble next to the sentence with the misspelled word. If all the underlined words are spelled correctly, choose "correct as is."

6. Ⓐ Meg <u>wonderd</u> if Pam were coming.

   Ⓑ <u>Perhaps</u> Tim could help them fix it.

   Ⓒ The <u>maid</u> cleaned the hotel room.

   Ⓓ correct as is

7. Ⓐ Zoo animals <u>frighten</u> my younger brother.

   Ⓑ The man was on <u>trial</u> for his crime.

   Ⓒ If we don't eat soon, I think I'll <u>starve</u>.

   Ⓓ correct as is

8. Ⓐ Scientists studied the <u>unknown</u> plant.

   Ⓑ My mom takes her <u>usaul</u> walk around the block.

   Ⓒ The explorers looked for the river's <u>source</u>.

   Ⓓ correct as is

9. Ⓐ The plumber must <u>repair</u> the pipes.

   Ⓑ This land is <u>flater</u> than that land.

   Ⓒ Jed has <u>been</u> working hard on his homework.

   Ⓓ correct as is

10. Ⓐ Paul is <u>convinced</u> that everyone will go.

    Ⓑ The police <u>observed</u> the robber leaving.

    Ⓒ Uncle Todd says Jon is his favorite <u>nephew</u>.

    Ⓓ correct as is

This is the end of the group-administered section of the Benchmark Assessment.

Name _____ **Date** _____ **Score** _____

Oral Fluency Assessment

Beth's three-year-old brother kicked and cried as she carried him toward the pool. Nick hated water, even bath water, but Beth wanted to show him that swimming could be fun. She sat at the pool's edge and encouraged him to put his feet in the water. Next she held his hand as he waded into the pool. The water came almost to his waist and he started to cry.	1–10 11–20 21–30 31–43 44–57 58–69 70–71
"Hey, Nick," she called, "try splashing me."	72–78
At first he slapped the water, barely making a tiny spray. But soon he was sloshing water all over. Then Beth suggested Nick try putting his face in, but he only dipped his chin into the water.	79–89 90–100 101–113 114–115
Beth ducked her head under the water and came up spouting water. "Can you do that?"	116–125 126–131
Nick's head went under, and he came up spluttering. Beth held him until he stopped sobbing.	132–141 142–147
"Come on, Nick, you can do it. Try again."	148–156
Soon Nick was putting his face in. Beth wanted him to try swimming, but he refused to lift his feet off the ground. Still, he had made a start. Beth thought he'd be swimming by the end of the summer.	157–168 169–180 181–192 193–196

READING RATE AND ACCURACY

Total Words Read: _____

Number of Errors: _____

Number of Correct Words _____

Read Per Minute (WPM): _____

Accuracy Rate: _____

(Number of Correct Words Read per Minute ÷ Total Words Read)

READING FLUENCY

	Low	Average	High
Decoding Ability	O	O	O
Pace	O	O	O
Syntax	O	O	O
Self-correction	O	O	O
Intonation	O	O	O

Oral Fluency Assessment

Beth's three-year-old brother kicked and cried as she carried him toward the pool. Nick hated water, even bath water, but Beth wanted to show him that swimming could be fun. She sat at the pool's edge and encouraged him to put his feet in the water. Next she held his hand as he waded into the pool. The water came almost to his waist and he started to cry.

"Hey, Nick," she called, "try splashing me."

At first he slapped the water, barely making a tiny spray. But soon he was sloshing water all over. Then Beth suggested Nick try putting his face in, but he only dipped his chin into the water.

Beth ducked her head under the water and came up spouting water. "Can you do that?"

Nick's head went under, and he came up spluttering. Beth held him until he stopped sobbing.

"Come on, Nick, you can do it. Try again."

Soon Nick was putting his face in. Beth wanted him to try swimming, but he refused to lift his feet off the ground. Still, he had made a start. Beth thought he'd be swimming by the end of the summer.

Expository Writing Prompt

Directions for Writing

Think about different jobs people have. Write about a job you would like to have in the future. Tell what you would do in the job and why you would like to have that job. Tell as much as you can about the job

Checklist

You will earn the best score if you

- think about a job you would like to have.
- think about your audience as you plan your writing.
- write so that your ideas will help the reader understand why you would like this job.
- have an opening paragraph that gets the attention of readers.
- write paragraphs that have a topic sentence and focus on related ideas.
- use transition words to go from one idea to another.
- avoid words and phrases that are overused.
- delete ideas that are not important.
- write more sentences and longer sentences when you revise.
- read your writing after you finish and check for mistakes.

Name _____ Date _____ Score _____

Comprehension

Read the following story. Then answer questions 1–10 relating to the story. You may look back at the story to find the answers.

Samatar stood on deck as the ship sailed slowly into New York Harbor. Before him was the Statue of Liberty. He had read about it in books. In the pictures, it had looked small. Here it towered over him. The statue was a lady dressed in a long flowing dress. She was holding a torch high in the air. It was a greenish color that was pretty but new to his eyes. His mother had told him to watch for the statue. That would mean their long ocean voyage was close to an end.

He breathed a sigh of relief. Samatar had thought the trip to America would be an adventure. Instead, he had been seasick most of the trip. At first, he was afraid that the waves would sink the ship. Soon he was too sick to care. He spent most of the trip in bed, moaning and wishing for the voyage to end. His younger sister, Awa, had laughed at him. She loved the motion of the boat. Awa could not believe her brother was not enjoying the trip as much as she was.

Comprehension (continued)

Now they were about to land. Around him, people crowded onto the deck to catch their first glimpse of their new home. Many of them had tears in their eyes. Some wept freely. Nearby, his father pulled his mother close. His mother rarely let his father out of her sight these days. Samatar tried to push away the thoughts of those bad days when his father had gone into hiding during the war. They had no idea if he was safe. They wondered if they would see him again. One night, he just showed up at their house. They packed all they could. Then came their long, scary journey to escape.

What would America be like? Samatar wondered. *Would he find friends?* He had learned some English words on the ship. Still, the language was strange. *Would he ever be able to talk to people?* Uncle Guleed would meet them. He had a small apartment they would all squeeze into. He and Awa would sleep on the floor. This would have to do until his parents found jobs. Then they would get a place of their own. But this was better than living in the midst of a war. And best of all, his family was whole again. Samatar raced to join his family before the ship landed at Ellis Island.

Comprehension (continued)

1. This story is mostly about

Ⓐ a boy and his family arriving in America.

Ⓑ things that happened on a boy's ocean voyage.

Ⓒ what it is like to live in a small, crowded apartment.

Ⓓ why people come to America from other places.

2. Where is the ship arriving?

Ⓐ Chesapeake Bay

Ⓑ Miami

Ⓒ Cape Cod

Ⓓ New York Harbor

3. How is the Statue of Liberty different from what Samatar has seen in books?

Ⓐ It is holding a torch.

Ⓑ It is greenish.

Ⓒ It towers overhead.

D It wears a flowing gown.

4. Why does Samatar not enjoy the voyage?

Ⓐ He is afraid of what will happen when they get to America.

Ⓑ He is growing tired of his little sister's behavior.

Ⓒ He is seasick from the rocking of the boat.

Ⓓ He is ashamed that he is learning English so slowly.

5. Which of these happened first?

Ⓐ Samatar's father goes into hiding.

Ⓑ The ship arrives in America.

Ⓒ The family packs their belongings.

Ⓓ There is a war in Samatar's country.

GO ON

Comprehension (continued)

6. Why is the family leaving their country?

Ⓐ They have jobs waiting for them in America.

Ⓑ They miss Samatar's uncle too much.

Ⓒ They are getting away from the war.

Ⓓ They have always wanted to travel.

7. Why does Samatar's mother keep his father in view most of the time?

Ⓐ She is afraid he may have fallen off the ship.

Ⓑ She missed him when he was in hiding.

Ⓒ She knows he is the only one in the family who knows English.

Ⓓ She worries that he will become seasick if she cannot see him.

8. Where had Samatar learned some English?

Ⓐ on the ship

Ⓑ at school

Ⓒ at home

Ⓓ from television

9. Where will the family live when they arrive in America?

Ⓐ in a farmhouse

Ⓑ in an apartment

Ⓒ in a mobile home

Ⓓ in a hotel

10. From the story, you can tell that

Ⓐ Samatar would like to be back home.

Ⓑ Samatar wants to find a job.

Ⓒ Samatar's family will fly to America next time.

Ⓓ Samatar loves his family.

GO ON

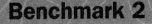

Name _____ Date _____ Score _____

Comprehension

Read the following selection. Then answer questions 1–10 relating to the selection. You may look back at the selection to find the answers.

In Kenya, night after night, some elephants head deep underground. Herds line up to enter the caves of Mount Elgon. The elephants walk in one by one. They have done this for many years. Nowhere else in the world do elephants go underground.

Scientists wondered about this strange behavior. They checked out the caves during the daytime while the elephants were gone. Mount Elgon, formed by an extinct volcano, is full of caves. Forests on both sides hide the caves.

Inside one cave they saw that elephants had widened the cave walls. This comes from years of digging at them with their tusks. The scientists also found a clue as to why the elephants go to the caves—they are looking for salt. Elephants need salt to live.

Many African elephants live in the savannah, a flat, grassy plain. The elephants get the salt they need from the grasses, trees, and roots they eat. But the elephants that live near Mount Elgon dwell in the forests. Heavy rains wash the salt from the trees and plants. If they do not have the right amount of salt in their diets, the elephants would not last long in this hot climate.

Comprehension (continued)

Salt keeps water in an elephant's body. Grown elephants can weigh as much as eight thousand pounds. They need a lot of food, water, and salt to stay alive. Most elephants eat between one hundred sixty and three hundred fifty pounds of food each day. To find and eat this much food, elephants spend most of the day eating. They need salt the same way they need water. If they do not get it from food they eat, they search for it.

For years, adult elephants have taught their babies to go into these caves in search of salt. But how do elephants find their way in the dark? They do not have good eyesight, even in the daylight. They use their other senses to find their way. They have a very good sense of smell. They can hear well, too. They also have a great sense of touch.

In the dark caves, they feel their way along with their trunks. Adults lead the way. They feel the ground in front of them before they take a step. The babies follow. They lean against their mother or hold on to her with their trunks. Inside the cave, the elephants use their tusks to scrape chunks of salt from the wall. Then they chew up the salt chunks. When they are done, they head back up the trail and into the forest.

Comprehension (continued)

1. This story is mostly about

   Ⓐ elephant behavior near Mount Elgon.

   Ⓑ how elephants find their way to a cave.

   Ⓒ how Mount Elgon was formed.

   Ⓓ salt formations inside of caves.

2. Mount Elgon is located in

   Ⓐ Europe.

   Ⓑ South America.

   Ⓒ Asia.

   Ⓓ Africa.

3. How are these elephants different from most other elephants?

   Ⓐ They live in the forest.

   Ⓑ They need more food.

   Ⓒ They can see in the dark.

   Ⓓ They need less water.

4. How much food do most elephants eat every day?

   Ⓐ between 160 and 350 calories

   Ⓑ between 16 and 35 pounds

   Ⓒ between 1600 and 3500 ounces

   Ⓓ between 160 and 350 pounds

5. Why do elephants need salt?

   Ⓐ to keep water in their bodies

   Ⓑ to make grass taste better

   Ⓒ to keep their skin smooth

   Ⓓ to get water out of their bodies

GO ON

Comprehension (continued)

6. Which sense is poorest in elephants?

Ⓐ hearing

Ⓑ touch

Ⓒ smell

Ⓓ sight

7. How have the elephants widened the cave walls?

Ⓐ by leaning against them

Ⓑ by pushing them with their trunks

Ⓒ by digging at them with their tusks

Ⓓ by kicking them with their hind legs

8. Why do the adults go into the cave first?

Ⓐ to be sure there are no lions

Ⓑ to lead their babies to salt

Ⓒ to be sure the floor won't cave in

Ⓓ to break up the rock for the babies

9. From the selection, you can tell that

Ⓐ elephants eat lots of other animals.

Ⓑ elephants are good at finding what they need to live.

Ⓒ forest elephants eat less than savannah elephants.

Ⓓ forest elephants only come out at night.

10. Which of the following would be a good title for this selection?

Ⓐ "Cave-Dwelling Elephants"

Ⓑ "How Elephants on the Savannah Live"

Ⓒ "Forest Elephants Meet their Needs"

Ⓓ "How Elephants See"

Vocabulary

Read each item. Fill in the bubble for the answer you think is correct.

1. Briefly means

   Ⓐ for a short time.

   Ⓑ friendly.

   Ⓒ without looking.

   Ⓓ cleanly.

2. Disturb is the base word in disturbing. Disturbing means

   Ⓐ respecting.

   Ⓑ traveling.

   Ⓒ troubling.

   Ⓓ laughing.

3. Biology means

   Ⓐ the study of space.

   Ⓑ the study of history.

   Ⓒ the study of rocks.

   Ⓓ the study of living things.

4. What word means about the same as anxious?

   Ⓐ happy

   Ⓑ calm

   Ⓒ nervous

   Ⓓ twisted

5. What word means about the same as vanish?

   Ⓐ jump

   Ⓑ disappear

   Ⓒ walk

   Ⓓ arrive

Vocabulary (continued)

6. What word means the opposite of <u>enormous</u>?

Ⓐ old   Ⓒ huge

Ⓑ ugly   Ⓓ tiny

7. Which word BEST completes both sentences?

My dog ___ when it gets too hot.

These are my new ___.

Ⓐ pants   Ⓒ hides

Ⓑ shorts   Ⓓ shoes

8. Which word BEST completes both sentences?

We heard a great ___ last night.

A metal ___ went around the tree.

Ⓐ record   Ⓒ band

Ⓑ concert   Ⓓ strap

9. A foul <u>odor</u> came from the swamp. <u>Odor</u> means

Ⓐ animal.   Ⓒ taste.

Ⓑ bug.   Ⓓ smell.

10. The old horse was very <u>gentle</u> with children. <u>Gentle</u> means

Ⓐ calm.   Ⓒ fast.

Ⓑ nervous.   Ⓓ bored.

Grammar, Usage, and Mechanics

Read each question. Fill in the bubble beside the answer in each group that is correct. If none of the answers is correct, choose the last answer, "none of the above."

1. Which sentence is written correctly?

(A) We went to Salt Lake City for Thanksgiving.

(B) We went to Salt Lake city for Thanksgiving.

(C) We went to Salt Lake City for thanksgiving.

(D) none of the above

2. Which sentence is written incorrectly?

(A) Here is what I brought: pop, candy, and videos.

(B) These are examples of citrus fruit: Oranges, grapefruit, lemons, and limes.

(C) You must choose your favorite color: pink, purple, blue, or green.

(D) none of the above

3. Which sentence is written correctly?

(A) Homer is supposed to have written The Odyssey.

(B) Homer is supposed to have written the Odyssey.

(C) Homer is supposed to have written "the odyssey."

(D) none of the above

4. Which sentence is written incorrectly?

(A) "Spare me!" shouted the prisoner.

(C) Sue said "We will try again later."

(B) "I do not like mushrooms," said Bobby.

(D) none of the above

5. Which sentence is written correctly?

(A) Ben's happiest memories are of the time he spent in school.

(B) Ben's most happiest memories are of the time he spent in school.

(C) Ben's most happier memories are of the time he spent in school.

(D) none of the above

GO ON

Grammar, Usage, and Mechanics (continued)

6. Which sentence is written correctly?

Ⓐ Frank or Ella know the answer.

Ⓑ Frank and Ella knows the answer.

Ⓒ Frank or Ella knows the answer.

Ⓓ none of the above

7. Which sentence is written correctly?

Ⓐ He is carrying a bag in they hand.

Ⓑ He is carrying a bag in him hand.

Ⓒ He is carrying a bag in their hand.

Ⓓ none of the above

8. Which sentence is written <u>incorrectly</u>?

Ⓐ Though he tried hard, Julio's team lost.

Ⓑ When we go out to eat, Sheila does not eat much.

Ⓒ Aaron fixes dinner even though he was not hungry.

Ⓓ none of the above

9. Which sentence contains a compound predicate?

Ⓐ A cow and a goat wandered down the trail.

Ⓑ It took four days to finish the job.

Ⓒ The puppy stopped and smelled the flower.

Ⓓ none of the above

10. Which sentence contains a dependent clause?

Ⓐ Mrs. Hart wants to write a play about her family.

Ⓑ She carries a pack on her back and a book under her arm.

Ⓒ You will sleep if you drink warm milk.

Ⓓ none of the above

Spelling

Read each group of words. Only one of the words is spelled correctly. Fill in the bubble under the word that is spelled correctly.

1. staroge   storage   stroage   storaje
   Ⓐ   Ⓑ   Ⓒ   Ⓓ

2. degre   deegre   dergree   degree
   Ⓐ   Ⓑ   Ⓒ   Ⓓ

3. jogging   joging   jogginng   joggin
   Ⓐ   Ⓑ   Ⓒ   Ⓓ

4. fatsen   fastin   fasten   festen
   Ⓐ   Ⓑ   Ⓒ   Ⓓ

5. lawen   lawne   lanw   lawn
   Ⓐ   Ⓑ   Ⓒ   Ⓓ

GO ON

Spelling (continued)

In each sentence, look for the underlined word that is spelled incorrectly. Focus on just the underlined word. Fill in the bubble next to the sentence with the misspelled word. If all the underlined words are spelled correctly, choose "correct as is."

6. Ⓐ The <u>casheir</u> gave us the wrong change.

   Ⓑ Monday is <u>laundry</u> day at our house.

   Ⓒ Sometimes Leah is <u>impatient</u> with her little brother.

   Ⓓ correct as is

7. Ⓐ Avery learned a new <u>chord</u> on his guitar.

   Ⓑ The queen chose a <u>jewel</u> for her crown.

   Ⓒ The hikers found pieces of <u>pertrified</u> wood.

   Ⓓ correct as is

8. Ⓐ Liam needed his parents' <u>approval</u> to join the team.

   Ⓑ My little sister can be a real <u>nuisance</u>!

   Ⓒ Semir's brother is a <u>junour</u> in high school.

   Ⓓ correct as is

9. Ⓐ At the pool, Pedro likes to <u>plunge</u> right into the water.

   Ⓑ The friends made up after their <u>quarrell</u>.

   Ⓒ The hotel <u>provides</u> breakfast every morning.

   Ⓓ correct as is

10. Ⓐ The builder gave us an <u>estimate</u> for our new house.

   Ⓑ Visitors need a passport to cross the <u>border</u>.

   Ⓒ Do you have something to <u>occupy</u> yourself while you wait?

   Ⓓ correct as is

STOP **This is the end of the group-administered section of the Benchmark Assessment.**

Name _____ **Date** _____ **Score** _____

Oral Fluency Assessment

On vacation one day, Andy and his dad visited a small	1–11
pretzel factory. It was exciting and fun to watch enormous	12–21
machines stir the dough in big bowls.	22–28
The dough was made into a long rope called a "noodle."	29–39
The noodles were twisted and flipped by another machine.	40–48
It made the dough into pretzel shapes. These moved along	49–58
to a large pot of water. Dipping the pretzels gave them a	59–70
crunchy texture. It helped the salt stick, too.	71–78
In the next room, Andy smelled the pretzels baking.	79–87
He liked watching the trays slide into one end of the oven.	88–99
Then he watched the baked pretzels come out on the other	100–110
side.	111
But the best part came at the end of the tour where Andy	112–124
made his own pretzel. A woman in a white apron, wearing a	125–136
hair net, showed him how.	137–141
First, they rolled the dough into a long rope. Then, they	142–152
shaped the rope into an oval design, and crossed the ends of	153–164
the rope. They twisted them over and laid them on the oval.	165–176
Andy couldn't believe how easy it was. In front of him	177–187
was his very own pretzel. Buying a bag of pretzels to eat	188–199
on the way home was great, too!	200–206

READING RATE AND ACCURACY

Total Words Read: _____

Number of Errors: _____

Number of Correct Words

Read Per Minute (WPM): _____

Accuracy Rate: _____

(Number of Correct Words Read per
Minute ÷ Total Words Read)

READING FLUENCY

	Low	Average	High
Decoding Ability	○	○	○
Pace	○	○	○
Syntax	○	○	○
Self-correction	○	○	○
Intonation	○	○	○

Oral Fluency Assessment

On vacation one day, Andy and his dad visited a small pretzel factory. It was exciting and fun to watch enormous machines stir the dough in big bowls.

The dough was made into a long rope called a "noodle." The noodles were twisted and flipped by another machine. It made the dough into pretzel shapes. These moved along to a large pot of water. Dipping the pretzels gave them a crunchy texture. It helped the salt stick, too.

In the next room, Andy smelled the pretzels baking. He liked watching the trays slide into one end of the oven. Then he watched the baked pretzels come out on the other side.

But the best part came at the end of the tour where Andy made his own pretzel. A woman in a white apron, wearing a hair net, showed him how.

First, they rolled the dough into a long rope. Then, they shaped the rope into an oval design, and crossed the ends of the rope. They twisted them over and laid them on the oval.

Andy couldn't believe how easy it was. In front of him was his very own pretzel. Buying a bag of pretzels to eat on the way home was great, too!

Name _____ Date _____ Score _____

Comprehension

Read the following story. Then answer questions 1–10 relating to the story. You may look back at the story to find the answers.

For a long time, I was too sick to care that my hair fell out in clumps. Soon I was bald, but so were most of the others in the hospital cancer ward with me. We were all struggling to get well. Looks did not matter to us. But I am done with chemotherapy now. Today I start back to school.

It's hard enough starting middle school. It's worse when you've missed the first few months of school. I wonder if my friends have forgotten me. When I was first in the hospital, lots of them came to visit. As the months dragged on, hardly anyone came. The past few months, Dara was the only one who visited. She's the only one who's seen me bald. She didn't seem to mind. In fact, she brought me a scarf when I was still in the hospital. She showed me ways to tie it around my head. Then she held up a mirror so I could see my reflection. It was the first time I had studied myself in the mirror since starting chemotherapy. I have to say that it was pretty depressing.

"Don't worry, Angel," she said. "Your hair will grow back."

Comprehension (continued)

She's right. Still, it will take a long time. Anyway, today is the day I go back to school. I'm already a little late because I've been standing here in front of the mirror. I am trying to tie the headscarf over the peach fuzz on my head. I wish I'd asked Dara to come over and help me with the scarf. Somehow it doesn't look as nice as when she did it.

Dad drives me to school. As I'm getting out of the car, I spot Dara coming toward me. She's wearing a scarf wrapped around her head.

"Hey, Angel," she says, "I got permission to skip homeroom to help you find your first class."

As I follow her through the building, I glance in the other classrooms along the way. Everywhere I look I notice headscarves. When Dara sees me staring at the scarves, she gestures toward her head and smiles. "I thought it would make it easier for you on your first day back. Just think, you're responsible for a new fashion trend."

I smile back. It's a relief to know I won't be the only one walking around with my head wrapped today.

Comprehension (continued)

1. This story is mostly about

   Ⓐ a girl learning to tie a headscarf.

   Ⓑ what it is like to be in the hospital.

   Ⓒ a girl's recovery from cancer.

   Ⓓ how hard it is to be in middle school.

2. Why has Angel missed so much school?

   Ⓐ She has been sick.

   Ⓑ She is new in town.

   Ⓒ She is very smart.

   Ⓓ She has few friends.

3. Why does Angel think her friends have forgotten her?

   Ⓐ She does not get cards from them any more.

   Ⓑ They do not come to visit her as much.

   Ⓒ They do not recognize her without hair.

   Ⓓ She does not see them when she arrives at school.

4. On her first day of school, Angel's hair is like

   Ⓐ silk.

   Ⓑ steel wool.

   Ⓒ banana peel.

   Ⓓ peach fuzz.

5. How does Angel get to school on her first day back?

   Ⓐ Dara walks with her.

   Ⓑ Her dad drives her.

   Ⓒ She takes the bus.

   D She rides her bike.

Comprehension (continued)

6. Who comes to Angel as she arrives at school?

   Ⓐ the principal

   Ⓑ her friend Dara

   Ⓒ the school nurse

   Ⓓ her dad

7. Why are the other students wearing scarves?

   Ⓐ to help Angel feel better

   Ⓑ to be part of the newest fashion

   Ⓒ to practice tying headscarves

   Ⓓ to show school spirit

8. Dara helps Angel in all of these ways EXCEPT

   Ⓐ teaching her to tie a headscarf.

   Ⓑ skipping homeroom to find her first class.

   Ⓒ helping her with math homework.

   Ⓓ getting the other students to wear scarves.

9. A word you could use to describe Dara is

   Ⓐ funny.

   Ⓑ energetic.

   Ⓒ athletic.

   Ⓓ kind.

10. From this story, you know that

   Ⓐ Angel is completely cured of cancer.

   Ⓑ Dara is an excellent student.

   Ⓒ Angel has many friends at school.

   Ⓓ Angel's teachers help her catch up.

GO ON

Name _____ Date _____ Score _____

Comprehension

Read the following selection. Then answer questions 1–10 relating to the selection. You may look back at the selection to find the answers.

Many people enjoy skydiving. That is jumping out of a plane with a parachute. Other people would like to try it. However, they might not be able to afford the cost. Some do not want to fall that far. These people try BASE jumping.

In BASE jumping, people use a parachute. However, they do not jump out of planes. They jump from a bridge, a building, or a cliff. The initials *BASE* come from words that describe the main places used for jumps. *B* stands for building. *A* is for antenna. *S* is for span and *E* for Earth.

The *B* is easy to understand. Tall buildings make good places for jumping. Antennas are high towers. Jumpers should only pick towers that are not in use. Towers that are being used are much too dangerous. Spans are rounded on top. Things like domes or arches would be spans. Bridges are also spans. The last letter stands for Earth. It means any natural features. These would be things such as cliffs.

Wherever people plan to jump, they need to think about a lot of things. The first problem is finding a safe place. Jumpers need to plan their landing spots carefully.

GO ON

Comprehension (continued)

Buildings or other places that do not have open spaces around them are not good choices. Jumpers need to look for anything nearby. They do not want to hurt themselves or harm their parachutes as they fall and land. Some people like to pick places where others can watch them jump. They need space for the people to stand. It must be a place that does not get in the way of their jump.

Another problem jumpers have is that they need to get permission to jump. Most of the places jumpers choose are owned by others. Many people do not want jumpers on their land. They worry that jumpers might get hurt. Some jumpers break the law. They jump without permission. This is never the right thing to do. It is not fair to the property owners. Also, depending on where the jump is, it can be against the law.

Safety is another problem. BASE jumping is a dangerous sport. Jumpers need special parachutes. When they jump, they are very close to the ground. They cannot fall like skydivers do. Their chutes must open much faster then those skydivers use. Since jumpers do not have much time, they must be sure that their chutes work well. If they are careful, BASE jumpers can have lots of fun.

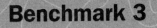
Comprehension (continued)

1. This story is mostly about

Ⓐ how a parachute works.

Ⓑ how to save money on a parachute.

Ⓒ what skydiving feels like.

Ⓓ an unusual activity.

2. The S in BASE stands for

Ⓐ silk.

Ⓑ span.

Ⓒ space.

Ⓓ sky.

3. A canyon would be an example of

Ⓐ Building.

Ⓑ Antenna.

Ⓒ Span.

Ⓓ Earth.

4. BASE jumpers are concerned about all of these problems EXCEPT

Ⓐ having to pay a lot for fuel.

Ⓑ finding a safe place to jump.

Ⓒ getting permission to jump.

Ⓓ making sure their chutes work.

5. How are BASE jumpers like skydivers?

Ⓐ Both are in freefall when they jump.

Ⓑ Neither requires a lot of space to jump.

Ⓒ Both jumpers need parachutes

Ⓓ Neither costs very much money.

Comprehension (continued)

6. Why do BASE jumpers chutes open more quickly than a skydiver's?

    Ⓐ The BASE jumper's chute is made of different material.

    Ⓑ The BASE jumper is falling more quickly than the skydiver.

    Ⓒ The BASE jumper is closer to the ground than the skydiver.

    Ⓓ The BASE jumper's chute is much larger than the skydiver's.

7. Which of these would be a good choice for BASE jumping?

    Ⓐ the antenna for the radio station across town

    Ⓑ a tall cliff with a meadow below it

    Ⓒ a 40-story apartment building in the city

    Ⓓ in the middle of a ranch in Texas

8. Property owners do not want BASE jumpers on their property mostly because

    Ⓐ the jumpers do not have any money.

    Ⓑ the owners do not like jumpers.

    Ⓒ the property will be damaged.

    Ⓓ the jumpers might get hurt.

9. Which of these is not a reason you need lots of space for your landing area?

    Ⓐ so you will not hit anything when you land

    Ⓑ so the airplane has enough room to land

    Ⓒ so other people can watch you jump

    Ⓓ so you will not damage your chute when you land

10. BASE jumpers are probably people who

    Ⓐ make friends easily.   Ⓒ like taking risks.

    Ⓑ enjoy going to the movies.   Ⓓ studied hard in school.

Vocabulary

Read each item. Fill in the bubble for the answer you think is correct.

1. <u>Dislike</u> means

  Ⓐ sing.

  Ⓑ hate.

  Ⓒ love.

  Ⓓ trust.

2. <u>Life</u> is the base word in <u>lifeless</u>. <u>Lifeless</u> means

  Ⓐ alive.

  Ⓑ young.

  Ⓒ dead.

  Ⓓ kind.

3. <u>Democracy</u> means

  Ⓐ government by voting.

  Ⓑ many people in one place.

  Ⓒ walking to a distant place.

  Ⓓ finding something by accident.

4. What word means about the same as <u>muttered</u>?

  Ⓐ shouted

  Ⓑ whispered

  Ⓒ cried

  Ⓓ mumbled

5. What word means about the same as <u>contented</u>?

  Ⓐ satisfied

  Ⓑ annoyed

  Ⓒ angry

  Ⓓ confused

GO ON

Vocabulary (continued)

6. What word means the opposite of <u>exciting</u>?

Ⓐ new

Ⓑ dull

Ⓒ silly

Ⓓ long

7. Which word BEST completes both sentences?

My mother will ___ the walls.

Is this today's ___?

Ⓐ paint   Ⓒ repair

Ⓑ paper   Ⓓ mail

8. Which word BEST completes both sentences?

Mr. Rose paid a parking ___.

The worker did a ___ job.

Ⓐ fee   Ⓒ fine

Ⓑ great   Ⓓ good

9. Be sure to get your parents' <u>approval</u> for the trip. <u>Approval</u> means

Ⓐ address.   Ⓒ packages.

Ⓑ permission.   Ⓓ names.

10. We received an <u>appeal</u> for donations. <u>Appeal</u> means

Ⓐ request   Ⓒ notice.

Ⓑ ticket.   Ⓓ demand.

Grammar, Usage, and Mechanics

Read each question. Fill in the bubble beside the answer in each group that is correct. If none of the answers is correct, choose the last answer, "none of the above."

1. Which sentence is written correctly?

   Ⓐ She attends Four Corners school on Federal Street.

   Ⓑ She attends Four Corners school on Federal street.

   Ⓒ She attends four Corners School on Federal Street.

   Ⓓ none of the above

2. Which sentence is written <u>incorrectly</u>?

   Ⓐ There are three primary colors, red, yellow, and blue.

   Ⓑ There are two things I always carry: a comb and ten dollars.

   Ⓒ She only likes three people: her aunt, her mom, and her dad.

   Ⓓ none of the above

3. Which sentence is written correctly?

   Ⓐ The Wizard of Oz will only be showing for a week.

   Ⓑ "The wizard of oz" will only be showing for a week.

   Ⓒ The wizard of oz will only be showing for a week.

   Ⓓ none of the above

4. Which sentence is written correctly?

   Ⓐ "We have to go home now," Mother said.

   Ⓑ We have to go home now Mother said.

   Ⓒ "We have to go home now, Mother said."

   Ⓓ none of the above

5. Which sentence is written correctly?

   Ⓐ The brown cow lazily chewed its food.

   Ⓑ The brown cow lazy chewed its food.

   Ⓒ The brown cow lazier chewed its food.

   Ⓓ none of the above

Grammar, Usage, and Mechanics (continued)

6. Which sentence is written <u>incorrectly</u>?

   Ⓐ Was it Ted or Tommy who saw it?

   Ⓑ A parent or teacher am coming with us.

   Ⓒ My mom or my dad took out the trash.

   Ⓓ none of the above

7. Which sentence is written correctly?

   Ⓐ My sister and I both like sardines.

   Ⓑ My sister and me both like sardines.

   Ⓒ My sister and him both like sardines.

   Ⓓ none of the above

8. Which sentence is written <u>incorrectly</u>?

   Ⓐ The cat catches the mouse as it left its hole.

   Ⓑ Johnny was hit hard in yesterday's game.

   Ⓒ Amber loves to play outside when the snow falls.

   Ⓓ none of the above

9. Which sentence contains a compound subject?

   Ⓐ Everyone wore costumes to school for the play.

   Ⓑ The neighbors bought a new lawnmower and a new rake.

   Ⓒ Ducks and geese spend the winter at the lake.

   Ⓓ none of the above

10. Which sentence contains a dependent clause?

   Ⓐ The bus went to the next town but Jerry stayed at home.

   Ⓑ The butterfly was caught by a spider.

   Ⓒ Runners eat pretzels when they need salt.

   Ⓓ none of the above

Spelling

Read each group of words. Only one of the words is spelled correctly. Fill in the bubble under the word that is spelled correctly.

1. portest   protset   protest   pretost
   Ⓐ   Ⓑ   Ⓒ   Ⓓ

2. stareo   steroe   sterrio   stereo
   Ⓐ   Ⓑ   Ⓒ   Ⓓ

3. equally   eqaully   equaly   equilly
   Ⓐ   Ⓑ   Ⓒ   Ⓓ

4. pulbic   public   poblic   publick
   Ⓐ   Ⓑ   Ⓒ   Ⓓ

5. main   mian   moin   naim
   Ⓐ   Ⓑ   Ⓒ   Ⓓ

GO ON

Spelling (continued)

In each sentence, look for the underlined word that is spelled incorrectly. Focus on just the underlined word. Fill in the bubble next to the sentence with the misspelled word. If all the underlined words are spelled correctly, choose "correct as is."

6. Ⓐ Dad gave Mom a <u>diamond</u> ring.

   Ⓑ Paula's parents <u>rent</u> that house.

   Ⓒ Humans <u>braethe</u> air to stay alive.

   Ⓓ correct as is

7. Ⓐ Do you <u>agree</u> with his answer?

   Ⓑ We stood in a <u>shelter</u> during the storm.

   Ⓒ Look both ways before you step off the <u>curb</u>.

   Ⓓ correct as is

8. Ⓐ Try to <u>avoid</u> the icy patches.

   Ⓑ This <u>level</u> of the mall has a food court.

   Ⓒ The police solved the <u>mistery</u>.

   Ⓓ correct as is

9. Ⓐ A cheetah is a <u>rapid</u> runner.

   Ⓑ Nancy can put this <u>puzzel</u> together.

   Ⓒ The sign said, "Do not <u>disturb</u>."

   Ⓓ correct as is

10. Ⓐ The explorers found a <u>pasage</u> through the mountains.

   Ⓑ One problem for the poor in many places is <u>hunger</u>.

   Ⓒ The farmers found <u>plentiful</u> water in the valley.

   Ⓓ correct as is

STOP This is the end of the group-administered section of the Benchmark Assessment.

Name _____ Date _____ Score _____

Oral Fluency Assessment

In January, people who celebrate Christmas have to get	1–9
rid of their trees. People who buy live trees can plant them.	10–21
And those with artificial trees can store them until next year.	22–32
But that still leaves piles of leftover trees.	33–40
Getting rid of all these trees can be a problem. Some	41–51
towns recycle them. The trees are shredded and used as	52–61
mulch. The mulch is placed around the bottom of plants	62–71
in parks.	72–73
There's another way to get rid of trees. Germany uses	74–83
this idea all around the country. Trees are taken to the zoo.	84–95
They are fed to the animals.	96–101
Many animals like to eat pine trees. Sheep, camels, and	102–111
deer all love to eat the leftover trees. But the biggest eater	112–123
is the elephant. Elephants can eat as many as five trees at a	124–136
time for a meal.	137–140
Not only do animals enjoy eating the trees, but it is	141–151
also good for them. The oils in pine trees are good for an	152–164
animal's digestion. Pine bark can help asthma and high blood	165–174
pressure. It not only works for animals. It works for people.	175–185
Who knows? Maybe one day, people won't recycle their trees	186–195
any more. They will eat them instead.	196–202

READING RATE AND ACCURACY

Total Words Read: _____

Number of Errors: _____

Number of Correct Words

Read Per Minute (WPM): _____

Accuracy Rate: _____

(Number of Correct Words Read per
Minute ÷ Total Words Read)

READING FLUENCY

	Low	Average	High
Decoding Ability	O	O	O
Pace	O	O	O
Syntax	O	O	O
Self-correction	O	O	O
Intonation	O	O	O

Oral Fluency Assessment

In January, people who celebrate Christmas have to get rid of their trees. People who buy live trees can plant them. And those with artificial trees can store them until next year. But that still leaves piles of leftover trees.

Getting rid of all these trees can be a problem. Some towns recycle them. The trees are shredded and used as mulch. The mulch is placed around the bottom of plants in parks.

There's another way to get rid of trees. Germany uses this idea all around the country. Trees are taken to the zoo. They are fed to the animals.

Many animals like to eat pine trees. Sheep, camels, and deer all love to eat the leftover trees. But the biggest eater is the elephant. Elephants can eat as many as five trees at a time for a meal.

Not only do animals enjoy eating the trees, but it is also good for them. The oils in pine trees are good for an animal's digestion. Pine bark can help asthma and high blood pressure. It not only works for animals. It works for people. Who knows? Maybe one day, people won't recycle their trees any more. They will eat them instead.

Name _____ **Date** _____ **Score** _____

Comprehension

Read the following story. Then answer questions 1–10 relating to the story. You may look back at the story to find the answers.

The lights were dim. The audience was quiet and was paying close attention to the curtain that was about to open. Mike knew he was supposed to be totally quiet, too. Out on the stage, Kevin Kane was calmly walking around, getting ready to say his first lines. Mike was standing in the wings, where the curtain met the edge of the stage.

When the curtain went up and the play started, Mike could not help murmuring Kevin's lines along with the older actor. "Someday I'll leave this town," said Kevin in a clear voice. "Someday I'll leave this town," whispered Mike.

"That will be me someday," Mike said to himself as Kevin paused, listening to another actor recite her lines in the play. Mike had tried out for the lead role in this play. But Kevin Kane was older, and frankly, better. Even Mike knew that. "He has more presence," the drama teacher had said. "Kevin also has more experience. Your time will come, Mike."

Comprehension (continued)

Still, at least the teacher had asked Mike to be Kevin's understudy. It was an important job, and Mike felt good that the teacher chose him. That was why Mike knew all of Kevin's lines. If Kevin could not do a show for any reason, Mike could step right in. Mike hated to admit it, but he wished that Kevin would catch a cold for at least one night of the play.

Mike also had a part of his own in the play. It was a very small part, but he always did his best. Hearing his cue, he tugged his costume into place and ran out into the bright lights. *Don't look at the audience,* he reminded himself, *speak clearly.* "The train is here!" he shouted. Turning, he ran back off the stage.

The curtain came down. That was the end of the first act. It was also the end of Mike's part in the play. He sighed as he changed out of his costume. Then he looked at himself in the mirror. In the spring, the school would put on another play. "I can always try out for the lead in the spring play. And Kevin graduates this year, so next year is mine." His face stared solemnly back at him. "Maybe this spring Kevin and I can trade places." His face split into a big grin. Then he walked out of the theater to look for his family.

Comprehension (continued)

1. This story is mostly about

   Ⓐ a school play.

   Ⓑ two friends competing.

   Ⓒ how to be an actor.

   Ⓓ a boy's dream.

2. Kevin Kane could best be described as

   Ⓐ nervous.

   Ⓑ confident.

   Ⓒ energetic.

   Ⓓ boastful.

3. Why was Mike supposed to be totally quiet?

   Ⓐ He had no lines in the play.

   Ⓑ He might distract the audience.

   Ⓒ He was trying to sneak up on Kevin.

   Ⓓ He did not have permission to be there.

4. The drama teacher thinks that

   Ⓐ Kevin will catch a cold one night.

   Ⓑ Kevin will be Mike's understudy.

   Ⓒ Mike will have a chance someday.

   Ⓓ Mike will forget his lines too easily.

5. What will happen to Kevin?

   Ⓐ He will become an actor someday.

   Ⓑ He will play the lead in the spring.

   Ⓒ He will graduate this year.

   Ⓓ He will come down with a cold.

GO ON

Comprehension (continued)

6. When will the next play be?

  Ⓐ the spring

  Ⓑ the next month

  Ⓒ the next week

  Ⓓ the winter

7. What does Mike hope will happen in the spring?

  Ⓐ Kevin will be Mike's understudy.

  Ⓑ The teacher will choose a new play.

  Ⓒ His family will move to a new school.

  Ⓓ Someone will help Mike learn his lines.

8. Which of these happens last?

  Ⓐ Mike's part in the play is over.

  Ⓑ Mike waits in the wings.

  Ⓒ Mike looks in the mirror.

  Ⓓ Mike tries out for the lead.

9. To whom is Mike speaking at the end of the story?

  Ⓐ himself

  Ⓑ Kevin

  Ⓒ the drama teacher

  Ⓓ the audience

10. In this story, the author creates a sense of

  Ⓐ expectation on Mike's part.

  Ⓑ anxiety in Kevin.

  Ⓒ concern by the teacher about the play.

  Ⓓ celebration because the play was a success.

Name _____ **Date** _____ **Score** _____

Comprehension

**Read the following selection. Then answer questions
1–10 relating to the selection. You may look back at the
selection to find the answers.**

One of the most amazing things about oak trees is that
they grow from tiny acorns. These acorns might be as small
as an inch long. And while many acorns fall, few of them turn
into trees. Only one of every ten thousand acorns will grow
into a tree.

Most oak trees do not start making acorns until they are
between twenty and fifty years old. By the time they are
seventy or eighty years old, they may make thousands of
acorns. Not all of these acorns are healthy. A tree needs a
lot of food and energy to produce strong acorns. Most oaks
are lucky if this happens once every few years. Usually oaks
grow good acorns once every four to ten years. But, of those
good ones, many still will not grow into trees.

Other things can affect how well acorns grow. Acorns
begin as small flowers in the spring. Cold or frost during this
time can kill them. Trees also need enough rain in the summer
for the small acorns to grow. These small acorns are called
nubbins. The nubbins on a tree will ripen by late summer.

GO ON

Comprehension (continued)

During the summer, the acorns have other problems. Insects called weevils drill holes in some of the acorns. They lay an egg in each hole. Then the eggs hatch. The young insects feed on the meat of the acorn. After the young insects have grown, they cut a new hole in the acorn. This hole lets the weevil escape. That acorn will not grow. It will soon dry up. Then it will fall from the tree. By the time fall comes, weevils will have ruined many acorns.

After the acorns fall, birds and deer eat many of the good ones. Squirrels also hide acorns. They store some of them in holes in trees. The acorns cannot grow in these holes. They also bury acorns in the ground. Some of these hidden acorns grow into trees, but many just rot.

Even after an acorn starts growing, it may not become an old oak. An animal might eat the young tree. A person might step on it. It is surprising that even one acorn turns into an oak tree. But some do. Once they take root, oaks may grow for hundreds of years. One oak in Maryland lived for more than four hundred sixty years. It must have come from a strong acorn!

Comprehension (continued)

1. This selection is mostly about

Ⓐ things that happen to acorns.

Ⓑ why animals like acorns.

Ⓒ the life cycle of an oak tree.

Ⓓ how weevils use acorns.

2. How many acorns grow into trees?

Ⓐ one in a thousand

Ⓑ one in ten

Ⓒ one in ten thousand

Ⓓ one in a million

3. Which of these is a reason for an oak tree to not produce acorns?

Ⓐ It was too warm in the springtime.

Ⓑ There was too much rain.

Ⓒ The tree got too much sun.

Ⓓ The tree is not old enough.

4. From this selection, you know that oak trees have

Ⓐ wood that is hard to cut.

Ⓑ leaves that stay green all year.

Ⓒ tiny flowers.

Ⓓ weak roots.

5. Which of these happens first?

Ⓐ A young weevil cuts a hole in the acorn.

Ⓑ An adult weevil lays an egg in a hole.

Ⓒ An adult weevil drills a hole in the acorn.

Ⓓ A young weevil eats the meat from an acorn.

GO ON

Comprehension (continued)

6. The inside of an acorn is called

    Ⓐ nubbin.

    Ⓑ meat.

    Ⓒ scale.

    Ⓓ weevil.

7. A weevil is most like a

    Ⓐ tree.

    Ⓑ beetle.

    Ⓒ rock.

    Ⓓ acorn.

8. Why do squirrels hide acorns?

    Ⓐ to keep them away from deer

    Ⓑ to grow new oak trees

    Ⓒ to eat during the winter

    Ⓓ to give weevils a place for eggs

9. The selection says there was a very old oak tree in

    Ⓐ Maryland.

    Ⓑ New York.

    Ⓒ Florida.

    Ⓓ Michigan.

10. From the selection, you know that

    Ⓐ acorns are a squirrel's favorite food.

    Ⓑ most acorns are eaten by young weevils.

    Ⓒ deer like to eat small oak trees.

    Ⓓ some oak trees are older than people.

Vocabulary

Read each item. Fill in the bubble for the answer you think is correct.

1. <u>Scientist</u> means

   Ⓐ a school that teaches science.

   Ⓑ a building where people study science.

   Ⓒ a project that uses science.

   Ⓓ a person who studies science.

2. <u>Appear</u> is the base word in <u>disappear</u>. <u>Disappear</u> means

   Ⓐ equal.

   Ⓑ vanish.

   Ⓒ control.

   Ⓓ defend.

3. <u>Native</u> means

   Ⓐ a boat with sails.

   Ⓑ a forest in a warm place.

   Ⓒ a person from a place.

   Ⓓ a city from long ago.

4. What word means about the same as <u>rim</u>?

   Ⓐ center

   Ⓑ entry

   Ⓒ edge

   Ⓓ bottom

5. What word means about the same as <u>locate</u>?

   Ⓐ lose

   Ⓑ find

   Ⓒ acquire

   Ⓓ damage

GO ON

Vocabulary (continued)

6. What word means the opposite of <u>distant</u>?

Ⓐ nearby

Ⓑ far away

Ⓒ tall

Ⓓ tree-covered

7. Which word BEST completes both sentences?

The ____ is still in the can of paint.

The deer walked through the ____.

Ⓐ can   Ⓒ woods

Ⓑ brush   Ⓓ jar

8. Which word BEST completes both sentences?

We looked in both ____.

What do the ____ say?

Ⓐ paths   Ⓒ words

Ⓑ directions   Ⓓ boxes

9. Kim cannot find anything in her <u>untidy</u> room. <u>Untidy</u> means

Ⓐ large.   Ⓒ messy.

Ⓑ clean.   Ⓓ dark.

10. Each <u>nation</u> sent a team to the Olympics. <u>Nation</u> means

Ⓐ town.   Ⓒ city.

Ⓑ country.   Ⓓ state.

Grammar, Usage, and Mechanics

Read each question. Fill in the bubble beside the answer in each group that is correct. If none of the answers is correct, choose the last answer, "none of the above."

1. Which sentence is written <u>incorrectly</u>?

   Ⓐ Brian was also known as Wonder Boy.

   Ⓑ They speak Japanese at Home and English at School.

   Ⓒ Orlando, Florida is the home of Disney World.

   Ⓓ none of the above

2. Which sentence is written correctly?

   Ⓐ Bring these on the hike water, a snack, and sunscreen.

   Ⓑ Bring these on the hike: Water, a snack, and sunscreen.

   Ⓒ Bring these on the hike: water, a snack, and sunscreen.

   Ⓓ none of the above

3. Which sentence is written correctly?

   Ⓐ There is always a copy of the magazine <u>Smithsonian</u> at our house.

   Ⓑ There is always a copy of the magazine smithsonian at our house.

   Ⓒ There is always a copy of the "magazine Smithsonian" at our house.

   Ⓓ none of the above

4. Which sentence is written correctly?

   Ⓐ "I want to ride the roller coaster again" shouted Lynn!

   Ⓑ "I want to ride the roller coaster again!" shouted Lynn.

   Ⓒ "I want to ride the roller coaster again"! shouted Lynn.

   Ⓓ none of the above

5. Which sentence is written <u>incorrectly</u>?

   Ⓐ My tallest friend reached up to the top shelf.

   Ⓑ Louise tied the laces on her shoe more tighter.

   Ⓒ Juanita is the friendliest person I know.

   Ⓓ none of the above

GO ON

Grammar, Usage, and Mechanics (continued)

6. Which sentence is written correctly?

Ⓐ She and I is the players the team wanted.

Ⓑ She and I was the players the team wanted.

Ⓒ She and I were the players the team wanted.

Ⓓ none of the above

7. Which sentence is written correctly?

Ⓐ You are going to make that men laugh.

Ⓑ You are going to make those man laugh.

Ⓒ You are going to make that man laugh.

Ⓓ none of the above

8. Which sentence is written correctly?

Ⓐ Nadia does not get discouraged when the work was difficult.

Ⓑ Nadia does not get discouraged when the work is difficult.

Ⓒ Nadia did not get discouraged when the work is difficult.

Ⓓ none of the above

9. Which sentence contains a compound subject?

Ⓐ Cactus and large rocks were placed around the garden.

Ⓑ The phone doesn't seem to be working.

Ⓒ A strange bird came to the feeder yesterday afternoon.

Ⓓ none of the above

10. Which sentence contains a dependent clause?

Ⓐ Digging ditches is hard work.

Ⓑ The team wanted to win, so the coach had extra practice.

Ⓒ Danny painted a picture of a mountain scene.

Ⓓ none of the above

STOP

Spelling

Read each group of words. Only one of the words is spelled correctly. Fill in the bubble under the word that is spelled correctly.

1. macking   makin   makking   making
   Ⓐ   Ⓑ   Ⓒ   Ⓓ

2. chilly   chily   chilley   chelliy
   Ⓐ   Ⓑ   Ⓒ   Ⓓ

3. corwd   croud   crowd   crowt
   Ⓐ   Ⓑ   Ⓒ   Ⓓ

4. barfoot   barefoot   barefot   bairfoot
   Ⓐ   Ⓑ   Ⓒ   Ⓓ

5. scarecly   sarcely   scaircely   scarcely
   Ⓐ   Ⓑ   Ⓒ   Ⓓ

GO ON

Spelling (continued)

In each sentence, look for the underlined word that is spelled incorrectly. Focus on just the underlined word. Fill in the bubble next to the sentence with the misspelled word. If all the underlined words are spelled correctly, choose "correct as is."

6. Ⓐ The teacher wrote on the <u>chaklboard</u>.

   Ⓑ My friend goes to the <u>academy</u> of dance.

   Ⓒ The <u>subway</u> is the fastest way into town.

   Ⓓ correct as is

7. Ⓐ What <u>happens</u> next?

   Ⓑ We see an <u>ocasional</u> movie.

   Ⓒ Pete needs <u>film</u> for his camera.

   Ⓓ correct as is

8. Ⓐ The dog had <u>flease</u>.

   Ⓑ Give her a little <u>poke</u> to wake her up.

   Ⓒ My cat's <u>paws</u> were all muddy.

   Ⓓ correct as is

9. Ⓐ Sandy needs a <u>boost</u> to climb the tree.

   Ⓑ The police offered a <u>reward</u> for clues.

   Ⓒ Aunt Nell <u>returns</u> on the noon train.

   Ⓓ correct as is

10. Ⓐ Fill this <u>bucket</u> with water.

   Ⓑ The <u>police</u> helped the lost boy.

   Ⓒ You will <u>remian</u> here until we get back.

   Ⓓ correct as is

STOP This is the end of the group-administered section of the Benchmark Assessment.

Name _____ **Date** _____ **Score** _____

Oral Fluency Assessment

As long as she could remember, Jill had always wanted	1–10
a pet. Every time Jill asked about owning a pet, her parents	11–22
told her the same thing: "Jill, I wish we lived in a house and	23–36
had a yard. Then we would get is a dog or cat for you, but	37–51
we can't have one where we are living now."	52–60
One day, on their way home from school, Jill and her	61–71
younger brother, Jay, stopped by their grandmother's house.	72–79
When they walked through the door, they were greeted by	80–89
joyful barks from an adorable, tiny brown dog.	90–97
"Gran, did you get a dog?" Jill asked with hopeful	98–107
excitement. "No, honey, that's the Martins' dog, Ed. I am	108–117
watching him for a few hours. It would be difficult for me	118–129
to have a dog, Jill. I know you really want to have a pet	130–143
yourself, but I just don't see how it's possible."	144–152
"Can't we rent a dog or cat?" suggested Jay as he	153–163
petted Ed.	164–165
Jill and her grandmother laughed at the idea. Then	166–174
Mrs. Wilson stopped, her eyes brightened, and she smiled	175–183
and said, "That is not a bad idea, Jay! The animal shelter	184–195
has been looking for volunteers. Do you think you would	196–205
be interested?"	206–207

READING RATE AND ACCURACY

Total Words Read: _____

Number of Errors: _____

Number of Correct Words

Read Per Minute (WPM): _____

Accuracy Rate: _____

(Number of Correct Words Read per
Minute ÷ Total Words Read)

READING FLUENCY

	Low	Average	High
Decoding Ability	○	○	○
Pace	○	○	○
Syntax	○	○	○
Self-correction	○	○	○
Intonation	○	○	○

Oral Fluency Assessment

As long as she could remember, Jill had always wanted a pet. Every time Jill asked about owning a pet, her parents told her the same thing: "Jill, I wish we lived in a house and had a yard. Then we would get is a dog or cat for you, but we can't have one where we are living now."

One day, on their way home from school, Jill and her younger brother, Jay, stopped by their grandmother's house. When they walked through the door, they were greeted by joyful barks from an adorable, tiny brown dog.

"Gran, did you get a dog?" Jill asked with hopeful excitement. "No, honey, that's the Martins' dog, Ed. I am watching him for a few hours. It would be difficult for me to have a dog, Jill. I know you really want to have a pet yourself, but I just don't see how it's possible."

"Can't we rent a dog or cat?" suggested Jay as he petted Ed.

Jill and her grandmother laughed at the idea. Then Mrs. Wilson stopped, her eyes brightened, and she smiled and said, "That is not a bad idea, Jay! The animal shelter has been looking for volunteers. Do you think you would be interested?"

Expository Writing Prompt

Directions for Writing

Think about some outdoor places you have visited. They can be parks, a farm, the beach, or any other outdoor place that comes to mind. Write about the outdoor place you like best. Tell where the place is, what it looks like, and what you did there. Explain why you like this place so much.

Checklist

You will earn the best score if you

- think about your favorite outdoor place.
- think about your audience as you plan your writing.
- write so that your ideas will help the reader understand why you like this place.
- have an opening paragraph that gets the attention of readers.
- write paragraphs that have a topic sentence and focus on related ideas.
- use transition words to go from one idea to another.
- avoid words and phrases that are overused.
- delete ideas that are not important.
- write more sentences and longer sentences when you revise.
- read your writing after you finish and check for mistakes.

Name _____ Date _____ Score _____

Comprehension

Read the following story. Then answer questions 1–10 relating to the story. You may look back at the story to find the answers.

With her eyes squeezed shut, Sue tried to remember. She knew her teacher had explained a problem like this yesterday when they had reviewed for the test. Still, her mind stayed blank. Why was math always so hard for her?

Sitting like this, she could almost see Vanda's paper. Maybe if she wriggled over a bit in her seat and kept her eyes almost closed, Ms. Wilson would not notice. She could peer out through the small slit at the bottom of her eyes. She would not really cheat. She would just look at how Vanda did those problems. Once she saw that, she could probably figure it out for herself. No one would ever know she had peeked.

No one but you, Sue said to herself. She sighed. Then Ms. Wilson looked her way. Sue was glad she had not looked at Vanda's paper. She knew she had messed up a lot of the answers. She was not as glad when she got the test back the next day. She crumpled her paper and shoved it in her desk before anyone could see she failed another test—especially Vanda. As usual, Vanda had gotten every single problem right. Math was so easy for Vanda. Sue wished she knew Vanda's secret.

Comprehension (continued)

As she was leaving school, Ms. Wilson stopped her. "Sue," she said, "I wondered if you would like some extra help in math." When Sue nodded, she went on, "Vanda is willing to work with you. She's sure her mother wouldn't mind if you came over after school a few days a week. Would that be okay?"

Sue hesitated. She did not want Vanda to know how bad she was in math. Besides, she had soccer practice two nights a week. She never understood how she could be so good at soccer and so bad at math.

"Sue, why don't you think about it? And check with your parents."

Two days later, Sue was sitting at the table in Vanda's kitchen. When Sue didn't understand something, Vanda explained it differently until she did. At school, Sue was too embarrassed to ask Ms. Wilson to explain things a second time. Now she could ask as many questions as she wanted, and Vanda didn't seem to mind.

A few weeks later, Ms. Wilson handed back their math tests. Vanda glanced over, saw Sue's *C*, and gave her a thumbs up. It wasn't an *A* like Vanda had. Yet it was the best Sue had done all year. She had worked hard, and that made her proud.

GO ON

Comprehension (continued)

1. This story is mostly about
Ⓐ how to solve a math problem.
Ⓑ how math teachers help students.
Ⓒ how a girl improved in math.
Ⓓ how it is harder to learn out of class.

2. Why are Sue's eyes closed at the beginning of the story?
Ⓐ She is falling asleep.
Ⓑ She is trying to remember something.
Ⓒ She is pretending to be blind.
Ⓓ She is shielding her eyes from the sun.

3. What had happened in school the day before Sue's first test?
Ⓐ Sue had a soccer game.
Ⓑ Vanda had helped her study.
Ⓒ Ms. Wilson had a review.
Ⓓ The principal thought Sue had cheated.

4. Why is Sue glad she did not look at Vanda's paper?
Ⓐ She knew the teacher had been watching her.
Ⓑ She knew it was important not to cheat.
Ⓒ She knew Vanda was as bad at math as she was.
Ⓓ She knew Vanda was taking a different test.

5. Who would probably figure out that Sue had cheated?
Ⓐ her mother
Ⓑ Vanda's friend
Ⓒ the principal
Ⓓ the teacher

GO ON

Benchmark Assessment • Benchmark 5

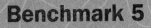

Comprehension (continued)

6. Which of these happened first?

Ⓐ Ms. Wilson stops Sue.

Ⓑ Sue crumples her paper.

Ⓒ Vanda looks at Sue's paper.

Ⓓ Sue sits in Vanda's kitchen.

7. Sue is all of these things EXCEPT

Ⓐ proud.

Ⓑ athletic.

Ⓒ hardworking.

Ⓓ dishonest.

8. Why does Vanda look at Sue's test?

Ⓐ to see her answers

Ⓑ to see her grade

Ⓒ to check her work

Ⓓ to compare tests

9. A good word to describe Vanda is

Ⓐ patient.

Ⓑ athletic.

Ⓒ foolish.

Ⓓ helpless.

10. Why is Sue proud at the end of the story?

Ⓐ She had earned her best grade all year.

Ⓑ She had gotten a better grade than Vanda.

Ⓒ She had scored two goals at soccer.

Ⓓ She had helped Vanda with soccer.

GO ON

Comprehension

Read the following selection. Then answer questions 1–10 relating to the selection. You may look back at the selection to find the answers.

Earthquakes occur every day. However, only the stronger ones are felt. An earthquake is the shaking of the ground. It is caused by energy released in Earth's crust.

Humans can cause small quakes. Some are caused by digging for minerals or drilling for oil. Damming water and removing natural gas from the ground have all caused them. The worst ones are caused by shifts in Earth's crust. The crust may bend, break, or snap. It may move to a new position. This movement travels out from these spots in waves. Some of these waves are so loud that we can hear them.

Many quakes happen along faults. These are places where Earth's crust is split or separated. The crust of Earth is weak there. The crust is cut into sections called plates. When these plates bump against each other or move on top of one another, it also causes earthquakes.

Quakes that happen under the ocean floor can cause tsunamis. These are huge waves that rush to the shore. They may travel more than five hundred miles per hour. They can be up to fifty feet high. If they hit an area with a lot of people or businesses, they cause major damage and deaths.

Comprehension (continued)

An earthquake may show that a volcano is about to erupt. Some quakes cause landslides. These landslides can be more harmful than what started them. Mud or dirt sliding down from high mountains can cover a whole town. Other dangers include holes in the ground, falling buildings, gas leaks, and fires. Major quakes can cause injury and death. They may also leave people homeless.

One way earthquakes are rated is by the Richter scale. This scale gives each quake a number. This data tells how strong the quake was. Most people can feel a number 2 quake. If it measures 6 or more, it is major. The worst ones measure 8 or more. The power of an earthquake can cover a large area. In big quakes, it can affect the whole planet. Not everyone will feel it, though.

People have tried different ways to predict earthquakes. Now people use machines that draw zigzag lines to show the shaking of the ground. They can tell where the quake started. They can tell what time it began. They know how long it lasted and how deep it was. Knowing when quakes are about to begin allows time to warn people. It can help saves lives.

GO ON

Comprehension (continued)

1. This selection is mostly about

Ⓐ tsunamis.

Ⓑ volcanoes.

Ⓒ earthquakes.

Ⓓ landslides.

2. The selection says that earthquakes occur

Ⓐ in the summer.

Ⓑ on land.

Ⓒ every day.

Ⓓ predictably.

3. Which human activity could cause an earthquake?

Ⓐ driving a car

Ⓑ building a house

Ⓒ cheering at a stadium

Ⓓ drilling for oil

4. Which of these would NOT cause an earthquake?

Ⓐ a big truck going down the street

Ⓑ tectonic plates bumping each other

Ⓒ removing natural gas from the ground

Ⓓ a buildup of water from a dam

5. Which of these causes the worst earthquakes?

Ⓐ digging for minerals

Ⓑ tsunamis

Ⓒ damming water

Ⓓ shifting plates

Comprehension (continued)

6. Which of these is true about a tsunami?

    Ⓐ It can avoid hitting any land.

    Ⓑ It can create a thousand foot wave.

    Ⓒ It has never killed anyone.

    Ⓓ It may travel five hundred miles per hour.

7. An earthquake is least likely to cause

    Ⓐ broken windows.

    Ⓑ falling buildings.

    Ⓒ flat tires on cars.

    Ⓓ holes in the ground.

8. Which of these does a machine used to measure earthquakes NOT show?

    Ⓐ when the next earthquake will be

    Ⓑ where an earthquake starts

    Ⓒ when an earthquake starts

    Ⓓ how deep an earthquake is

9. From this selection, you know that

    Ⓐ the author has been in a lot of earthquakes.

    Ⓑ more severe quakes rate higher on the Richter scale.

    Ⓒ earthquakes are harder to predict than they used to be.

    Ⓓ few earthquakes happen under the ocean.

10. Why do scientists try to predict earthquakes?

    Ⓐ to save lives and property

    Ⓑ to improve the Richter scale

    Ⓒ to test their equipment

    Ⓓ to prove mathematical formulas

Benchmark 5

Vocabulary

Read each item. Fill in the bubble for the answer you think is correct.

1. <u>Misuse</u> means

   Ⓐ use wrongly.

   Ⓑ like too much.

   Ⓒ move downward.

   Ⓓ lift quickly.

2. <u>Courage</u> is the base word in <u>encourage</u>. <u>Encourage</u> means

   Ⓐ to scare someone.

   Ⓑ to be surprised.

   Ⓒ to give confidence.

   Ⓓ to tell a story.

3. <u>Memorial</u> means

   Ⓐ a favor.

   Ⓑ a reminder.

   Ⓒ a motion.

   Ⓓ a prairie.

4. What word means about the same as <u>stumbled</u>?

   Ⓐ jumped

   Ⓑ walked

   Ⓒ ran

   Ⓓ tripped

5. What word means about the same as <u>chores</u>?

   Ⓐ jobs

   Ⓑ meetings

   Ⓒ naps

   Ⓓ friends

GO ON

Vocabulary (continued)

6. What word means the opposite of <u>difficult</u>?

Ⓐ challenging   Ⓒ easy

Ⓑ steep   Ⓓ narrow

7. Which word BEST completes both sentences?

The car ___ is always busy.

This ___ grows quickly.

Ⓐ plant   Ⓒ tree

Ⓑ factory   Ⓓ store

8. Which word BEST completes both sentences?

You will have to ___ for the race.

The ___ ride was fun.

Ⓐ practice   Ⓒ boar

Ⓑ bus   Ⓓ train

9. Smallpox is a <u>disease</u> that few people catch any more. <u>Disease</u> means

Ⓐ plant.   Ⓒ illness.

Ⓑ food.   Ⓓ excuse.

10. When my hands get <u>clammy</u>, I use a handkerchief. <u>Clammy</u> means

Ⓐ shaky.   Ⓒ tired.

Ⓑ strong.   Ⓓ moist.

Grammar, Usage, and Mechanics

Read each question. Fill in the bubble beside the answer in each group that is correct. If none of the answers is correct, choose the last answer, "none of the above."

1. Which sentence is written correctly?

   Ⓐ The Grand Canyon is in Arizona.

   Ⓑ The grand Canyon is in Arizona.

   Ⓒ The grand canyon is in Arizona.

   Ⓓ none of the above

2. Which sentence is written correctly?

   Ⓐ Aaron, Justine, Maria and Karen: are going to the movies today.

   Ⓑ Aaron and Justine: Maria, Karen are going to the movies today.

   Ⓒ Aaron: Justine, Maria and Karen are going to the movies today.

   Ⓓ none of the above

3. Which sentence is written <u>incorrectly</u>?

   Ⓐ We saw a play called <u>Easy Come, Easy Go</u>.

   Ⓑ "The Raven" is my favorite poem.

   Ⓒ A movie has been made out of the play "The Seagull."

   Ⓓ none of the above

4. Which sentence is written correctly?

   Ⓐ "Jose said, It isn't my turn yet."

   Ⓑ Jose said, "It isn't my turn yet.

   Ⓒ Jose said, It isn't my turn yet?

   Ⓓ none of the above

5. Which sentence is written correctly?

   Ⓐ The black dog is bigger than the white one.

   Ⓑ The black dog is more bigger than the white one.

   Ⓒ The black dog is most big than the white one.

   Ⓓ none of the above

GO ON

Grammar, Usage, and Mechanics (continued)

6. Which sentence is written correctly?

Ⓐ Luna and her brother go to the new elementary school.

Ⓑ Luna and her brother goes to the new elementary school.

Ⓒ Luna and her brother was going to the new elementary school.

Ⓓ none of the above

7. Which sentence is written <u>incorrectly</u>?

Ⓐ The grapes were too sour when I ate them.

Ⓑ I wore those gloves last winter.

Ⓒ Them is my favorite kinds of soup.

Ⓓ none of the above

8. Which sentence is written correctly?

Ⓐ The movie started after the previews are shown.

Ⓑ The movie starts after the previews were shown.

Ⓒ The movie started after the previews were shown.

Ⓓ none of the above

9. Which sentence contains a compound predicate?

Ⓐ The tide rose and flooded the marsh.

Ⓑ Look at the size of the apples on that tree.

Ⓒ The zoo parking lot was completely full.

Ⓓ none of the above

10. Which sentence contains a dependent clause?

Ⓐ You can go if you bring your sister.

Ⓑ My sister has a dog and a cat.

Ⓒ The photographer took a picture of the trees.

Ⓓ none of the above

Spelling

Read each group of words. Only one of the words is spelled correctly. Fill in the bubble under the word that is spelled correctly.

1. slippers   slipers   sllipers   slippirs
   Ⓐ   Ⓑ   Ⓒ   Ⓓ

2. giulty   guilty   guitly   giultey
   Ⓐ   Ⓑ   Ⓒ   Ⓓ

3. blod   bloode   bloud   blood
   Ⓐ   Ⓑ   Ⓒ   Ⓓ

4. paerl   pealr   pearl   peral
   Ⓐ   Ⓑ   Ⓒ   Ⓓ

5. stiars   stairs   staars   steirs
   Ⓐ   Ⓑ   Ⓒ   Ⓓ

GO ON

Spelling (continued)

In each sentence, look for the underlined word that is spelled incorrectly. Focus on just the underlined word. Fill in the bubble next to the sentence with the misspelled word. If all the underlined words are spelled correctly, choose "correct as is."

6. Ⓐ Be sure to read the next <u>chapter</u>.

   Ⓑ Building a house takes a lot of <u>labor</u>.

   Ⓒ The wood felt <u>smooth</u> and hard.

   Ⓓ correct as is

7. Ⓐ The butcher must <u>sharpen</u> his knife.

   Ⓑ Aunt Julie wants tea with <u>lemon</u>.

   Ⓒ Dad gave us <u>permision</u> to go.

   Ⓓ correct as is

8. Ⓐ Work hard and you will <u>succeed</u>.

   Ⓑ The park is in a <u>central</u> place.

   Ⓒ <u>Load</u> up the truck and let's go.

   Ⓓ correct as is

9. Ⓐ The football player wore a <u>helmet</u>.

   Ⓑ Those coins are <u>valauble</u>.

   Ⓒ Make a <u>chart</u> for the classroom.

   Ⓓ correct as is

10. Ⓐ There are <u>thrity</u> houses on this block.

    Ⓑ The old bridge is <u>unsafe</u>.

    Ⓒ The fire burned down to <u>ashes</u>.

    Ⓓ correct as is

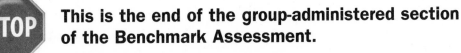

This is the end of the group-administered section of the Benchmark Assessment.

Name _____ Date _____ Score _____

Oral Fluency Assessment

It was 1717. The pirate Sam "Black Sam" Bellamy was headed for our coast. His ship, the *Bounty*, was loaded with treasure. Sam and his crew had stolen it from other ships. They thought they would all be rich!	1–10 11–21 22–32 33–39
Black Sam was worried. A storm was brewing. Black Sam tried to make it to land, but his luck had run out. The waves smashed the *Bounty*. The ship sank into the sea. Black Sam and his crew drowned. His treasure was lost.	40–49 50–63 64–74 75–82
Most people forgot all about Black Sam and his pirate ship filled with treasure. But not everyone forgot Black Sam's story. A boy named Barry Clifford grew up hearing about the pirate ship. In the 1970s, he decided to find the *Bounty*. Clifford searched for 15 years. Each year, he was disappointed.	83–92 93–101 102–111 112–123 124–132 133–134
Finally, in 1985, Clifford and his team found a large bell. It had the words "Bounty Gally 1716" written on it. This was the proof! Clifford had found the *Bounty*. Since then, Clifford and his team have found piles of gold coins, cannons, and guns. Clifford has also found everyday items like teapots and buttons. Many of these items are now in a museum. Black Sam's treasure has been found at last.	135–145 146–157 158–167 168–178 179–188 189–199 200–206

READING RATE AND ACCURACY

Total Words Read: _____

Number of Errors: _____

Number of Correct Words _____

Read Per Minute (WPM): _____

Accuracy Rate: _____

(Number of Correct Words Read per Minute ÷ Total Words Read)

READING FLUENCY

	Low	Average	High
Decoding Ability	○	○	○
Pace	○	○	○
Syntax	○	○	○
Self-correction	○	○	○
Intonation	○	○	○

Oral Fluency Assessment

It was 1717. The pirate Sam "Black Sam" Bellamy was headed for our coast. His ship, the *Bounty*, was loaded with treasure. Sam and his crew had stolen it from other ships. They thought they would all be rich!

Black Sam was worried. A storm was brewing. Black Sam tried to make it to land, but his luck had run out. The waves smashed the *Bounty*. The ship sank into the sea. Black Sam and his crew drowned. His treasure was lost.

Most people forgot all about Black Sam and his pirate ship filled with treasure. But not everyone forgot Black Sam's story. A boy named Barry Clifford grew up hearing about the pirate ship. In the 1970s, he decided to find the *Bounty*. Clifford searched for 15 years. Each year, he was disappointed.

Finally, in 1985, Clifford and his team found a large bell. It had the words "Bounty Gally 1716" written on it. This was the proof! Clifford had found the *Bounty*. Since then, Clifford and his team have found piles of gold coins, cannons, and guns. Clifford has also found everyday items like teapots and buttons. Many of these items are now in a museum. Black Sam's treasure has been found at last.

Name _____ Date _____ Score _____

Comprehension

Read the following story. Then answer questions 1–10 relating to the story. You may look back at the story to find the answers.

Lynn raced down the stairs, papers scattering as she ran. She was late again, but she needed to find her gym shoes. Her dad stood frowning, as Lynn stuffed loose papers in her backpack. She gave him a quick hug and dashed out the door. Luckily, the school bus had been stuck in traffic. Her dad didn't have to drive her to school.

At school, the principal said that if she were late again, Lynn would have detention. She had forgotten her history paper. Her math teacher complained that she could not check Lynn's answers because the paper was crumpled and torn. Lynn was disappointed in herself. She didn't know what to do.

When she got home from school, her dad was waiting for her with several empty boxes and some bags. "It's time to get organized," he said. Lynn followed her dad to her room. She did not know what to suggest.

"Let's start with the desk," he said. He grabbed a handful of papers. "Look through these to see what you need to keep."

They tossed out papers she did not need. Lynn was surprised at how many papers she had collected. Some were several years old.

GO ON

Comprehension (continued)

Next came the desk drawers. They dumped broken crayons, empty candy wrappers, and pens that did not write. When the drawers were empty, her father pulled containers out of the bags. Each item went into its own container—rubber bands, pens, paper clips, and markers.

With a feeling of satisfaction, Lynn started on the dresser drawers. Her father handed her two cardboard boxes. They were labeled "throw away" and "give away." Socks without mates and torn or stained clothes went into the first box. Clothes that did not fit or that she never wore went in the other. There were places in town where she could donate clothes.

They sorted everything under the bed. Then she tackled the closet. Soon shoes sat together in pairs, and clothes hung neatly on hangers. Lynn even cleaned out her purse and backpack.

"Now, Lynn," Dad said when they were done, "the trick is to keep it this way. When you use something, put it back where you got it. Throw away things that are broken. Don't shove them in drawers. For the next few weeks, we'll spend a little time on Saturday morning making sure things stay in order."

Lynn hugged him. "Thanks, Dad. I bet I'll be on time tomorrow. I can't wait for mom to get home tonight so I can show her what we did."

Comprehension (continued)

1. This story is mostly about

   Ⓐ how to improve a closet.

   Ⓑ giving old clothes to charity.

   Ⓒ a girl learning to organize.

   Ⓓ the importance of being on time.

2. At the beginning of the story, Lynn can be described as

   Ⓐ responsible.

   Ⓑ clever.

   Ⓒ disorganized.

   Ⓓ healthy.

3. Why was Lynn late when the story begins?

   Ⓐ She could not find her gym shoes.

   Ⓑ Her dad could not find the car keys.

   Ⓒ She was still doing her homework.

   Ⓓ The school bus was stuck in traffic.

4. Why is Lynn's dad frowning at the beginning of the story?

   Ⓐ He cannot find his keys.

   Ⓑ He sees Lynn running late.

   Ⓒ He knows that traffic is bad.

   Ⓓ He is not happy about his job.

5. What will happen to Lynn if she is late again?

   Ⓐ She will get detention.

   Ⓑ She will have extra assignments.

   Ⓒ Her dad will not be able to drive her.

   Ⓓ Her backpack will be lost.

GO ON

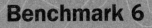
Comprehension (continued)

6. Which of these did Lynn and her dad do first?

  Ⓐ They sorted through her desk drawers.

  Ⓑ They gave Lynn's old clothes to charity.

  Ⓒ They threw out old papers.

  Ⓓ They went through things under the bed.

7. It appears as if Lynn used her desk drawer as a

  Ⓐ book shelf.

  Ⓑ trash can.

  Ⓒ sock drawer.

  Ⓓ chalk box.

8. What does Lynn's dad say is the trick about organizing?

  Ⓐ deciding what to throw out

  Ⓑ deciding what to give away

  Ⓒ keeping things where they belong

  Ⓓ having enough boxes that are big

9. Why does Lynn think she will be on time tomorrow?

  Ⓐ She will set her alarm correctly.

  Ⓑ She will fix lunch the night before.

  Ⓒ She will have a smaller breakfast.

  Ⓓ She will be able to find things.

10. From this story, we know that Lynn's dad

  Ⓐ is an organized person.

  Ⓑ does not know the principal.

  Ⓒ has an important job.

  Ⓓ will not help her any more.

GO ON

Name _____ Date _____ Score _____

Comprehension

Read the following selection. Then answer questions 1–10 relating to the selection. You may look back at the selection to find the answers.

People tend to fear quicksand. They worry that if they step into it, they will drown. In movies or cartoons, people sink deeper and deeper until the quicksand closes over their heads. The people flail their arms and legs as if that will stop them from sinking. But scientists who study quicksand say it is not as dangerous as it seems. The truth is that people cannot drown in it. This is because they will almost never sink farther down than chest level.

Getting out, though, can be tricky. Tugging someone out will not work. Quicksand is too powerful for that. It has such a strong power that it may end up pulling the person tugging into the mess, as well. Does that mean if you get stuck, you will never get out? Not if you know how quicksand works.

Quicksand is made of fine sand, salt water, and clay. This mixture gets thicker over time. Movement makes it turn to liquid. That is why people sink when they step on quicksand. The more movement there is, the more liquid quicksand becomes. If people struggle to get out, they sink deeper into it.

GO ON

Comprehension (continued)

Once a person is in the quicksand, it thickens up and becomes denser. That is why it is so hard to move. It is also why trying to pull people out is a bad idea. What would happen if you tried to pull someone out of dried cement? It would not work. In fact, it would be quite painful for them. The same is true with quicksand. Pulling one foot out takes as much force as lifting a car. Imagine the force it would take to pull out the rest of your body!

So what is the secret to getting out? What you need to do is wiggle your legs a little. This loosens the sand. It lets water flow down. This makes it more liquid. Do not move your legs fast. Do it slowly. If you move too much, you will sink again. And do not panic. Your body has a lower density than quicksand. It actually floats in quicksand. Therefore, there is no way you can go under all the way.

So remember to relax and move your legs slowly. Soon you will come to the surface. Better yet, stay away from quicksand!

Comprehension (continued)

1. This selection is mostly about

    Ⓐ scientists who study quicksand.

    Ⓑ how dangerous quicksand is.

    Ⓒ what quicksand is made of.

    Ⓓ how quicksand really works.

2. Which of these describes quicksand most accurately?

    Ⓐ It may be good for the health of some people.

    Ⓑ It actually tickles when you get stuck.

    Ⓒ It is not as dangerous as people think.

    Ⓓ It is rarely more than two feet deep.

3. Which of these is not an ingredient of quicksand?

    Ⓐ oxygen

    Ⓑ fine sand

    Ⓒ salt water

    Ⓓ clay

4. What happens to quicksand over time?

    Ⓐ It gets thinner.

    Ⓑ It gets thicker.

    Ⓒ It gets lighter.

    Ⓓ It gets darker.

5. Why is quicksand dangerous?

    Ⓐ It is very easy to drown in it.

    Ⓑ It has ingredients that are poisonous.

    Ⓒ It can cause diseases.

    Ⓓ It is hard to get out of.

GO ON

Comprehension (continued)

6. A person in quicksand will sink about as deep as the person's

   Ⓐ knee.

   Ⓑ hip.

   Ⓒ chest.

   Ⓓ head.

7. It is hard to move in quicksand because it

   Ⓐ hardens quickly once you fall in.

   Ⓑ is extremely slippery.

   Ⓒ gets denser once you fall in.

   Ⓓ is less dense than your body.

8. What is something you should do if you fall in quicksand?

   Ⓐ Do not move at all.

   Ⓑ Get somebody to pull on your arms.

   Ⓒ Thrash your arms and legs around.

   Ⓓ Wiggle your legs a little bit.

9. Why should you not pull somebody out of quicksand quickly?

   Ⓐ It might hurt them.

   Ⓑ You will fall in, too.

   Ⓒ Quicksand works too fast.

   Ⓓ They would not survive.

10. From this selection, you know that

   Ⓐ it is not possible to get out of quicksand.

   Ⓑ falling in quicksand probably will not kill you.

   Ⓒ quicksand does not smell very good.

   Ⓓ most quicksand is found in the desert.

Vocabulary

Read each item. Fill in the bubble for the answer you think is correct.

1. <u>Athletic</u> means

   Ⓐ almost finished.

   Ⓑ ready to leave.

   Ⓒ easily tired.

   Ⓓ good at sports.

2. <u>Skill</u> is the base word in <u>skillful</u>. <u>Skillful</u> means

   Ⓐ moving away from.

   Ⓑ having a special ability.

   Ⓒ without problems.

   Ⓓ not on time.

3. <u>Autograph</u> means

   Ⓐ a person's written name.

   Ⓑ prison.

   Ⓒ a place that is far away.

   Ⓓ thumb.

4. What word means about the same as <u>popular</u>?

   Ⓐ expensive

   Ⓑ liked

   Ⓒ crowded

   Ⓓ distant

5. What word means about the same as <u>crisp</u>?

   Ⓐ brisk

   Ⓑ warm

   Ⓒ muggy

   Ⓓ soggy

GO ON

Vocabulary (continued)

6. What word means the opposite of <u>grinned</u>?

Ⓐ frowned   Ⓒ smiled

Ⓑ joined   Ⓓ understood

7. Which word BEST completes both sentences?

Flour is made from ____.

This wood has a beautiful ____.

Ⓐ grain   Ⓒ finish

Ⓑ wheat   Ⓓ color

8. Which word BEST completes both sentences?

The park ___ needed paint.

The coach will ___ me if I am late.

Ⓐ bench   Ⓒ table

Ⓑ lamp   Ⓓ fire

9. The <u>fearless</u> knight never ran away.
<u>Fearless</u> means

Ⓐ brave.   Ⓒ smart.

Ⓑ foolish.   Ⓓ strong.

10. We all went to the wooden <u>lodge</u> to get warm.
<u>Lodge</u> means

Ⓐ tent.   Ⓒ diner.

Ⓑ cabin.   Ⓓ truck.

Grammar, Usage, and Mechanics

Read each question. Fill in the bubble beside the answer in each group that is correct. If none of the answers is correct, choose the last answer, "none of the above."

1. Which sentence is written correctly?

Ⓐ The Doctor specializes in heart surgery.

Ⓑ The doctor specializes in Heart Surgery.

Ⓒ The Doctor specializes in Heart Surgery.

Ⓓ none of the above

2. Which sentence is written correctly?

Ⓐ Three families live near ours: the Smiths, the Johnsons, and the Ramones.

Ⓑ Three families live near ours: The Smiths, the Johnsons, and the Ramones.

Ⓒ Three families live near ours the Smiths, the Johnsons, and the Ramones.

Ⓓ none of the above

3. Which sentence is written correctly?

Ⓐ Many people have read E.B. White's novel, "Charlotte's Web."

Ⓑ Many people have read E.B. White's novel, Charlotte's Web.

Ⓒ Many people have read E.B. White's novel, <u>Charlotte's Web</u>.

Ⓓ none of the above

4. Which sentence is written <u>incorrectly</u>?

Ⓐ Clark said "Let's go into the cave."

Ⓑ "It is too dark," said Milo.

Ⓒ Clark replied, "Don't be so scared."

Ⓓ none of the above

5. Which sentence is written correctly?

Ⓐ Their car went into the last turn too fastly.

Ⓑ Their car went into the last turn too faster.

Ⓒ Their car went into the last turn too fast.

Ⓓ none of the above

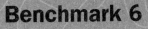

Grammar, Usage, and Mechanics (continued)

6. Which sentence is written <u>incorrectly</u>?

  Ⓐ Dena and Will are helping their mother.

  Ⓑ When dad called, Greg and Gary came running.

  Ⓒ Justin and Aaron are raking the leaves.

  Ⓓ none of the above

7. Which sentence is written correctly?

  Ⓐ Them crackers taste funny.

  Ⓑ These crackers taste funny.

  Ⓒ They crackers taste funny.

  Ⓓ none of the above

8. Which sentence is written <u>incorrectly</u>?

  Ⓐ Grandmother will call me when she needed a ride.

  Ⓑ When I went to school, I rode a bus.

  Ⓒ One time, the bus nearly hit me when it passed.

  Ⓓ none of the above

9. Which sentence contains a compound predicate?

  Ⓐ The restaurant opens at six o'clock in the morning.

  Ⓑ Horses ran around the field or nibbled the grass.

  Ⓒ The meeting will take place in the auditorium.

  Ⓓ none of the above

10. Which sentence contains a dependent clause?

  Ⓐ Mr. Nichols had to shovel snow several times last winter.

  Ⓑ My mother likes the park when the pond is frozen.

  Ⓒ The hardware store is just down the street.

  Ⓓ none of the above

Spelling

Read each group of words. Only one of the words is spelled correctly. Fill in the bubble under the word that is spelled correctly.

1. flod   fleod   floode   flood
    - Ⓐ   Ⓑ   Ⓒ   Ⓓ

2. sall   sela   sale   saile
    - Ⓐ   Ⓑ   Ⓒ   Ⓓ

3. limbs   lims   libms   lmibs
    - Ⓐ   Ⓑ   Ⓒ   Ⓓ

4. kicted   kicked   kikked   kickid
    - Ⓐ   Ⓑ   Ⓒ   Ⓓ

5. pirde   prode   preide   pride
    - Ⓐ   Ⓑ   Ⓒ   Ⓓ

Spelling (continued)

In each sentence, look for the underlined word that is spelled incorrectly. Focus on just the underlined word. Fill in the bubble next to the sentence with the misspelled word. If all the underlined words are spelled correctly, choose "correct as is."

6. Ⓐ The apple <u>blossoms</u> are out already.

   Ⓑ It <u>snowed</u> for three days in a row.

   Ⓒ Rain washed the <u>topsiol</u> away.

   Ⓓ correct as is

7. Ⓐ Fall <u>evenings</u> are chilly.

   Ⓑ There is too much <u>spice</u> in this soup.

   Ⓒ Put your <u>napkin</u> in your lap.

   Ⓓ correct as is

8. Ⓐ Let's <u>continue</u> this tomorrow.

   Ⓑ The <u>athalete</u> played three sports.

   Ⓒ Those socks are really <u>dirty</u>.

   Ⓓ correct as is

9. Ⓐ There was a <u>shortige</u> of food during the war.

   Ⓑ Close the <u>gate</u> when you leave.

   Ⓒ <u>Traffic</u> was backed up on Main Street.

   Ⓓ correct as is

10. Ⓐ The sailor told us a strange <u>tale</u>.

    Ⓑ Dad is the store <u>manageer</u> here.

    Ⓒ That movie was <u>shown</u> last week.

    Ⓓ correct as is

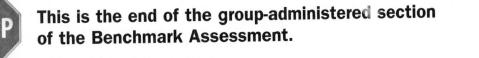

STOP **This is the end of the group-administered section of the Benchmark Assessment.**

Name _____ **Date** _____ **Score** _____

Oral Fluency Assessment

The circus was in town, and Tony's dad had agreed to take all of the boys on Saturday. But Brett had a problem. He was afraid of clowns. He didn't mention it to his friends, but that night, he told his dad.	1–12 13–25 26–37 38–42
The following afternoon, Brett's dad took Brett to the circus grounds. There they met Mr. Johnson. Brett was surprised to discover that Mr. Johnson was a clown. *He looks like an ordinary man*, Brett thought to himself.	43–51 52–60 61–71 72–79
"Many kids are frightened by clowns," Mr. Johnson said. "Let me show you something."	80–88 89–93
He led them into a dressing room. He covered his face with white makeup, drew on black eyebrows, and painted an enormous red circle around his mouth. This made him look scary. Still, Brett remembered it was only Mr. Johnson.	94–104 105–114 115–124 125–133
Mr. Johnson told Brett that every clown had special style of makeup. "If you look closely, you'll see that each clown is different and unique."	134–143 145–155 156–158
That Saturday, Brett went to the circus with his friends. When the clowns came out, Brett was frightened at first. Then he saw a familiar and friendly face. It was Mr. Johnson. Brett was able to relax and enjoy the circus.	159–168 169–178 179–190 191–199

READING RATE AND ACCURACY

Total Words Read: _____

Number of Errors: _____

Number of Correct Words

Read Per Minute (WPM): _____

Accuracy Rate: _____

(Number of Correct Words Read per Minute ÷ Total Words Read)

READING FLUENCY

	Low	Average	High
Decoding Ability	○	○	○
Pace	○	○	○
Syntax	○	○	○
Self-correction	○	○	○
Intonation	○	○	○

Oral Fluency Assessment

The circus was in town, and Tony's dad had agreed to take all of the boys on Saturday. But Brett had a problem. He was afraid of clowns. He didn't mention it to his friends, but that night, he told his dad.

The following afternoon, Brett's dad took Brett to the circus grounds. There they met Mr. Johnson. Brett was surprised to discover that Mr. Johnson was a clown. *He looks like an ordinary man*, Brett thought to himself.

"Many kids are frightened by clowns," Mr. Johnson said. "Let me show you something."

He led them into a dressing room. He covered his face with white makeup, drew on black eyebrows, and painted an enormous red circle around his mouth. This made him look scary. Still, Brett remembered it was only Mr. Johnson.

Mr. Johnson told Brett that every clown had special style of makeup. "If you look closely, you'll see that each clown is different and unique."

That Saturday, Brett went to the circus with his friends. When the clowns came out, Brett was frightened at first. Then he saw a familiar and friendly face. It was Mr. Johnson. Brett was able to relax and enjoy the circus.

Name _____ Date _____ Score _____

Comprehension

Read the following story. Then answer questions 1–10 relating to the story. You may look back at the story to find the answers.

Everyone knew that Juan came from a baseball family. His father loved baseball. His two brothers had played on teams since they were in the third grade. His mother had been a star softball player in high school and college. Juan had always liked watching games. But this year, he was not going to just watch anymore. He would also try out for a team.

The problem was that Juan was a little afraid. He knew he could not play very well. But he did not want to let his family down. When the day came for choosing players, Juan felt weak in the stomach. He decided he would do his best, but he was not sure he would make the team.

During the tryouts, Juan did not play well. He felt he had let his family down. Even so, the coach picked him for the team. Juan was happy he made the team, but was sorry he was not a good player.

After the tryout, Juan's mother gave him a big hug. She said she was proud that he tried so hard. Juan's brother, Brad, asked him, "Little brother, will you help me with my batting practice this afternoon?" They had a great time. Juan learned a lot about batting. Best of all, Brad said nothing about the tryout.

Comprehension (continued)

The next day, his other brother, Jerry, called Juan out into the back yard. "Hey, Juan, will you catch some of my pitches?" Jerry showed Juan some things about throwing and catching the ball. "Thanks for helping me," Juan said.

All summer the brothers and their dad practiced with Juan. They understood how he felt. They wanted him to play better. They didn't care if Juan was a star. They just wanted him to enjoy baseball as much as they did. Juan loved practicing with them and worked hard to get better.

Little by little, Juan improved at baseball. He felt better about himself. The family came to every game and cheered for him and the team. The coach let him play more and more, and by the end of the season, he was a starting player. Juan was never the star, and his team did not win many games, but he enjoyed playing baseball. And what was most important, he learned that his family cared for him very much, no matter what kind of baseball player he was.

Comprehension (continued)

1. This story is mostly about

   Ⓐ how to hit a baseball.

   Ⓑ how to choose a baseball team.

   Ⓒ how family support helps a boy.

   Ⓓ how much fun baseball is to play.

2. Which of these happens first?

   Ⓐ Juan helps Brad with batting practice.

   Ⓑ Juan's mother gives him a hug.

   Ⓒ Juan was a starting player on the team.

   Ⓓ Juan tries out for the baseball team.

3. Which of these is true about Juan's mother?

   Ⓐ She was the first female baseball player at her college.

   Ⓑ She does not really like baseball all that much.

   Ⓒ She played softball in high school and college.

   Ⓓ She is one of the coaches on Juan's team.

4. Why does Juan have a problem?

   Ⓐ He is afraid of getting hit with a baseball.

   Ⓑ He does not know the rules of the game.

   Ⓒ He does not have a glove and bat to use.

   Ⓓ He is not very good at playing baseball.

5. Why is Juan's mother proud?

   Ⓐ Her sons are all great players.

   Ⓑ Juan has tried his best.

   Ⓒ Brad hit a home run.

   Ⓓ She threw the ball the farthest.

GO ON

Comprehension (continued)

6. You can conclude that Juan's brothers are

   Ⓐ good in school.

   Ⓑ older than Juan.

   Ⓒ good at other sports.

   Ⓓ hoping he joins their team.

7. How does Jerry help Juan?

   Ⓐ He tells the coach to make Juan a starter.

   Ⓑ He cheers for him during his first game.

   Ⓒ He shows him how to catch and throw.

   Ⓓ He teaches him to figure out how fast a pitch is.

8. How quickly does Juan improve at baseball?

   Ⓐ little by little

   Ⓑ right away

   Ⓒ over the course of years

   Ⓓ during the game

9. Why does Juan's family help him so much?

   Ⓐ They want him to be a star player.

   Ⓑ They want his team to win more.

   Ⓒ They want him to enjoy baseball.

   Ⓓ They want to start their own team.

10. From this story, you learn that

   Ⓐ even good players have to practice.

   Ⓑ Juan's parents met at a ball game.

   Ⓒ Brad is a better player than Jerry.

   Ⓓ the coach picked Juan last.

GO ON

Comprehension

Read the following selection. Then answer questions 1–10 relating to the selection. You may look back at the selection to find the answers.

The first Father's Day card was sent more than four thousand years ago. It was not like a card you could find in your local store. Still, it showed how a boy felt about his father. A young boy in Babylon wrote the card to his father. He did not have paper back then. So he carved the card in clay. He wished his father good health and a long life. The clay hardened. That is why we can still read his words now.

People have thanked their fathers through the years. It was not until the 1900s that a special day was set aside for fathers. There are a number tales about how it started. But many think Sonora Smart Dodd was the person who first had the idea.

She heard a talk about how vital mothers are. Her mother had died when she was young. Her dad had taken care of her and her five siblings. Sonora knew how hard that must have been for him. She wanted to do something to honor him. He had done so much for her.

Comprehension (continued)

She decided that there should be a day just for dads. By that time, Mother's Day was already being celebrated. She spoke with some groups in Washington. That is where she was living at the time. She hoped Father's Day would be the first Sunday in June. That was her father's birthday. But there was not enough time to get ready. Instead, it was held it on the third Sunday of June. That was June 19, 1910. Today that is considered the first Father's Day.

At first, people did not take to the idea. Over time, the special day was celebrated in more and more places. But it did not become a true holiday until 1972. In that year, Congress made the third Sunday in June a national holiday.

America is not the only country to have a day for dads. Father's Day is held in places around the world. Most of them hold it on different days.

People of all ages honor their dads on this day. Many people also thank grandpas and step dads. Some thank those men who have been like fathers to them. The one thing all these men share is simple. They have had a real effect on the lives of others.

Comprehension (continued)

1. This selection is mostly about

   Ⓐ how Father's Day came to be.

   Ⓑ the very first Father's Day card.

   Ⓒ Father's Day in other countries.

   Ⓓ what Father's Day means to people.

2. The first Father's Day card was unusual because it

   Ⓐ had a picture of an animal.

   Ⓑ was given to a president.

   Ⓒ told a funny story.

   Ⓓ was made of clay.

3. How do we know about the first Father's Day card?

   Ⓐ The card was written in English.

   Ⓑ The card, a clay tablet, still exists.

   Ⓒ The ancestors of the boy who sent the card retell his story.

   Ⓓ The father of the boy who sent the card was a famous man.

4. From this selection, you know that

   Ⓐ holidays are the same around the world.

   Ⓑ people did not think we needed Father's Day.

   Ⓒ fathers have been thanked through the years.

   Ⓓ Father's Day began in Europe.

5. Sonora Smart Dodd got her idea for Father's Day from

   Ⓐ a talk about how important mothers are.

   Ⓑ her five brothers and sisters.

   Ⓒ not knowing when her father's birthday was.

   Ⓓ reading about a young boy from Babylon.

GO ON

Comprehension (continued)

6. Which of these is true about Sonora Smart Dodd's mother?

   Ⓐ She raised six children by herself.

   Ⓑ She died when Dodd was young.

   Ⓒ She helped Dodd start Father's Day.

   Ⓓ She lived in Washington long ago.

7. Where did Sonora Smart Dodd live when she started Father's Day?

   Ⓐ North Carolina

   Ⓑ New York

   Ⓒ Florida

   Ⓓ Washington

8. Who made Father's Day a national holiday?

   Ⓐ Sonora Smart Dodd

   Ⓑ Jobe

   Ⓒ Ms. Dodd's father

   Ⓓ Congress

9. When was Father's Day first celebrated in the United States?

   Ⓐ 1972

   Ⓑ 1910

   Ⓒ 2000

   Ⓓ 1776

10. From the selection you learn that Father's Day

   Ⓐ began as a holiday for fathers and mothers.

   Ⓑ is always on the first Sunday in June.

   Ⓒ took a while to establish as a holiday.

   Ⓓ is only celebrated in a few countries.

Vocabulary

Read each item. Fill in the bubble for the answer you think is correct.

1. <u>Impolite</u> means
   - Ⓐ screen.
   - Ⓑ nice.
   - Ⓒ rude.
   - Ⓓ order.

2. <u>Thick</u> is the base word in <u>thickness</u>. <u>Thickness</u> means
   - Ⓐ burning.
   - Ⓑ moods.
   - Ⓒ action.
   - Ⓓ width.

3. <u>Uniform</u> means
   - Ⓐ a strong wall.
   - Ⓑ a special set of clothes.
   - Ⓒ a big book.
   - Ⓓ a special kind of school.

4. What word means about the same as <u>ancient</u>?
   - Ⓐ young
   - Ⓑ enormous
   - Ⓒ beautiful
   - Ⓓ old

5. What word means about the same as <u>gloomy</u>?
   - Ⓐ bright
   - Ⓑ cold
   - Ⓒ dark
   - Ⓓ warm

Vocabulary (continued)

6. What word means the opposite of <u>gradually</u>?

Ⓐ slowly   Ⓒ immediately

Ⓑ finally   Ⓓ partially

7. Which word BEST completes both sentences?

Where is the light ___?

We can ___ seats now.

Ⓐ switch   Ⓒ bulb

Ⓑ change   Ⓓ buy

8. Which word BEST completes both sentences?

The worker carried a ___.

Let's ___ some apples.

Ⓐ pick   Ⓒ shovel

Ⓑ bake   Ⓓ ladder

9. First we had to <u>convince</u> our father the trip was safe. <u>Convince</u> means

Ⓐ tease.   Ⓒ scare.

Ⓑ persuade.   Ⓓ embarrass.

10. That cheap bike was not such a <u>bargain</u>. <u>Bargain</u> means

Ⓐ repair job.

Ⓑ good purchase.

Ⓒ right size.

Ⓓ nice color.

Benchmark 7

Grammar, Usage, and Mechanics

Read each question. Fill in the bubble beside the answer in each group that is correct. If none of the answers is correct, choose the last answer, "none of the above."

1. Which sentence is written <u>incorrectly</u>?

  Ⓐ Abraham Lincoln's birthday is February 12.

  Ⓑ Labor Day is september 4 this year.

  Ⓒ On May 30, we celebrate Memorial Day.

  Ⓓ none of the above

2. Which sentence is written correctly?

  Ⓐ You have three choices, skiing, sledding, or tubing.

  Ⓑ You have three choices: skiing, sledding, or tubing.

  Ⓒ You have three choices. Skiing, sledding, or tubing.

  Ⓓ none of the above

3. Which sentence is written <u>incorrectly</u>?

  Ⓐ Sports Illustrated is a very popular magazine.

  Ⓑ My favorite film is <u>Peter Pan</u>.

  Ⓒ Jeff read <u>Where the Wild Things Are</u> many times.

  Ⓓ none of the above

4. Which sentence is written correctly?

  Ⓐ Mary asked "Where are we going?"

  Ⓑ Mary asked, "Where are we going"

  Ⓒ Mary asked, "Where are we going?"

  Ⓓ none of the above

5. Which sentence is written correctly?

  Ⓐ I read more slower when I need to pay attention.

  Ⓑ I read more slowly when I need to pay attention.

  Ⓒ I read more slow when I need to pay attention.

  Ⓓ none of the above

GO ON →

Grammar, Usage, and Mechanics (continued)

6. Which sentence is written correctly?

- Ⓐ Carl and I practice tennis every morning.
- Ⓑ Carl and I practices tennis every morning.
- Ⓒ Carl or I practice tennis every morning.
- Ⓓ none of the above

7. Which sentence is written <u>incorrectly</u>?

- Ⓐ Hal could not figure out them directions.
- Ⓑ These colors are better than those colors.
- Ⓒ Eva has a pair of those shoes.
- Ⓓ none of the above

8. Which sentence is written correctly?

- Ⓐ The rooster crows when dawn breaks.
- Ⓑ The rooster crows when dawn broke.
- Ⓒ The rooster crowed when dawn will break.
- Ⓓ none of the above

9. Which sentence contains a compound subject?

- Ⓐ Mail the packages when you go to the post office.
- Ⓑ This supermarket has a snack bar and a salad bar.
- Ⓒ Traffic was stopped because of an accident.
- Ⓓ none of the above

10. Which sentence contains a dependent clause?

- Ⓐ My father worries when we are late.
- Ⓑ We planted tree on Arbor Day.
- Ⓒ The neighbors could not go sledding so we stayed home.
- Ⓓ none of the above

Name _____ **Date** _____ **Score** _____

Oral Fluency Assessment

One day a mountain is still. The next day the top of	1–12
the mountain explodes! What is going on here? It is just a	13–24
volcano doing its thing.	25–28
The word volcano comes from the name of a small island.	29–39
Long ago, people living near the island believed it was the	40–50
home of a god. This god made new weapons for the god of	51–63
war. When the god was working, he threw hot lava and dust	64–75
into the air.	76–78
Today we know that gods don't cause volcanoes to erupt.	79–88
An eruption happens when lava and dust are forced out of	89–99
the volcano. They erupt because of the melted rock inside	100–109
them. This melted rock is lighter than solid rock. Some of	110–120
the melted rock pushes through openings in Earth's surface.	121–129
Then you have an eruption. The melted rock is called lava.	130–140
Some eruptions are bigger than others. The size of the	141–150
explosion depends on how thin or thick the melted rock is.	151–161
When the melted rock is thin and runny, the gas can escape	162–173
and the lava flows. If the melted rock is thick, gas can't	174–185
escape. Pressure builds up. Then the gases explode.	186–193

READING RATE AND ACCURACY

Total Words Read: _____

Number of Errors: _____

Number of Correct Words

Read Per Minute (WPM): _____

Accuracy Rate: _____

(Number of Correct Words Read per Minute ÷ Total Words Read)

READING FLUENCY

	Low	Average	High
Decoding Ability	O	O	O
Pace	O	O	O
Syntax	O	O	O
Self-correction	O	O	O
Intonation	O	O	O

Oral Fluency Assessment

One day a mountain is still. The next day the top of the mountain explodes! What is going on here? It is just a volcano doing its thing.

The word volcano comes from the name of a small island. Long ago, people living near the island believed it was the home of a god. This god made new weapons for the god of war. When the god was working, he threw hot lava and dust into the air.

Today we know that gods don't cause volcanoes to erupt. An eruption happens when lava and dust are forced out of the volcano. They erupt because of the melted rock inside them. This melted rock is lighter than solid rock. Some of the melted rock pushes through openings in Earth's surface. Then you have an eruption. The melted rock is called lava.

Some eruptions are bigger than others. The size of the explosion depends on how thin or thick the melted rock is. When the melted rock is thin and runny, the gas can escape and the lava flows. If the melted rock is thick, gas can't escape. Pressure builds up. Then the gases explode.

Expository Writing Prompt

Directions for Writing
Think about some characters you have read about in a book, seen in a movie or watched on television. Write a story about the character you like best. Describe the character and tell about the story, movie, or television show the character is in. Explain why you like the character so much.

Checklist
You will earn the best score if you

- think about that character you like so much.
- think about your audience as you plan your writing.
- write so that your ideas will help the reader understand why the character is so great.
- have an opening paragraph that gets the attention of readers.
- write paragraphs that have a topic sentence and focus on related ideas.
- use transition words to go from one idea to another.
- avoid words and phrases that are overused.
- delete ideas that are not important.
- write more and longer sentences when you revise.
- read your writing after you finish and check for mistakes.

Benchmark 1 Answer Sheets

Benchmark 1

Comprehension (continued)

1. This story is mostly about
   - Ⓐ how to decorate a plain white dress.
   - Ⓑ the best places to find blackberries.
   - ● a grandmother telling a story to a boy.
   - Ⓓ how painful it is to be stuck with thorns.

2. Where were the blackberry bushes?
   - ● at the edge of the woods
   - Ⓑ in Grandma's back yard
   - Ⓒ at the blackberry farm
   - Ⓓ in the middle of a field

3. Why were the berries smashed through a strainer?
   - Ⓐ to make the ink darker
   - Ⓑ to sweeten the juice
   - ● to remove the seeds
   - Ⓓ to put in the Vitamin C

4. What sounds like fun to Nick?
   - ● making ink from blackberries
   - Ⓑ making juice from a powder
   - Ⓒ putting a design on white cloth
   - Ⓓ writing a letter to his friend

5. Who was Grandma writing a letter to?
   - Ⓐ Nick
   - ● a friend
   - Ⓒ her sister
   - Ⓓ Nick's mother

GO ON

4 • Level 4   Benchmark Assessment • Benchmark 1

Benchmark 1

Benchmark 1

Comprehension (continued)

6. Where was Grandma allowed to use her ink?
   - Ⓐ upstairs
   - ● outside
   - Ⓒ at school
   - Ⓓ on cloth

7. Why does Grandma's sister scream?
   - Ⓐ She has caught Grandma disobeying her mother.
   - ● She sees that her new white dress has been ruined.
   - Ⓒ She got stuck with a blackberry thorn.
   - Ⓓ She is calling to somebody who is outside.

8. In the story, which of these cannot be made from blackberries?
   - Ⓐ juice
   - Ⓑ ink
   - Ⓒ hair dye
   - ● a dress

9. From the story, you know that
   - Ⓐ Nick's mother did not know the dress story.
   - Ⓑ Grandma's sister is still mad about the ruined dress.
   - Ⓒ Nick did not believe Grandma's story.
   - ● Grandma did not know she had grabbed her sister's dress.

10. A good title for this story would be
   - ● "Grandma's Blackberry Stories"
   - Ⓑ "Nick Writes a Letter"
   - Ⓒ "Grandma Disobeys Her Mother"
   - Ⓓ "Our Little Secret"

GO ON

Benchmark Assessment • Benchmark 1   Level 4 • **5**

Benchmark 1

Benchmark 1

Comprehension (continued)

1. This selection is mostly about
   - Ⓐ how the ancient Egyptians built their huge pyramids.
   - Ⓑ how one man can lift very heavy things without help.
   - Ⓒ how to carve fancy designs into large pieces of coral.
   - ● how one man proved he knew the Egyptians' secret.

2. How long did Ed Leedskalnin go to school?
   - Ⓐ until high school
   - ● until fourth grade
   - Ⓒ through college
   - Ⓓ through sixth grade

3. Which of these best describes Ed Leedskalnin?
   - Ⓐ an engineer with a lot of experience
   - ● an immigrant with little education
   - Ⓒ a scientist who studied the pyramids
   - Ⓓ a dreamer who wanted to go to Egypt

4. Ed probably learned about cutting stone from
   - Ⓐ his neighbor.
   - Ⓑ an engineer.
   - ● his father.
   - Ⓓ a family friend.

5. Why did the castle take so long to finish?
   - ● Ed did all of the work by himself.
   - Ⓑ Ed had to find lots of coral.
   - Ⓒ Ed had to figure out how to cut the coral.
   - Ⓓ Ed had to find other people to help.

GO ON

8 • Level 4   Benchmark Assessment • Benchmark 1

Benchmark 1

Benchmark 1

Comprehension (continued)

6. What did Ed do before he put up the castle walls?
   - Ⓐ He learned how to build a magnet.
   - Ⓑ He studied the pyramids of Egypt.
   - Ⓒ He discussed the job with some engineers.
   - ● He made many carvings inside.

7. What is in the center of the moon fountain?
   - Ⓐ a magnet
   - ● a pond
   - Ⓒ a moon
   - Ⓓ a chair

8. Why do some people think Ed used magnetic force to move the rocks?
   - ● He said something about matter being affected by magnetism.
   - Ⓑ All of the other possible explanations do not make as much sense.
   - Ⓒ Engineers have found magnets under the base of the castle.
   - Ⓓ He told his wife he was going to use magnets.

9. Which of these did Ed probably not use?
   - ● cranes   Ⓒ rollers
   - Ⓑ levers   Ⓓ magnets

10. From the selection, you know that
   - Ⓐ Ed was a very large and strong man.
   - Ⓑ the Egyptians used ramps to move rocks.
   - ● nobody has quite figured out how Ed moved the coral.
   - Ⓓ Ed did not know how to make carvings out of rock.

STOP

Benchmark Assessment • Benchmark 1   Level 4 • **9**

Benchmark 1

Benchmark Assessment • Benchmark 1   Level 4 • **117**

Benchmark 1 Answer Sheets

Vocabulary

Read each item. Fill in the bubble for the answer you think is correct.

1. Repay means
   - Ⓐ pay too late.
   - Ⓑ not pay.
   - ● pay back.
   - Ⓓ pay too much.

2. Clear is the base word in unclear. Unclear means
   - Ⓐ without any friends.
   - ● hard to understand.
   - Ⓒ almost empty.
   - Ⓓ not on time.

3. Geology means
   - Ⓐ the study of farming.
   - Ⓑ the study of weather.
   - Ⓒ the study of books.
   - ● the study of the Earth.

4. What word means about the same as odd?
   - Ⓐ usual
   - Ⓑ dim
   - ● strange
   - Ⓓ awake

5. What word means about the same as crouched?
   - Ⓐ stood
   - Ⓑ ran
   - Ⓒ cried
   - ● bent

GO ON ➡

10 • Level 4   Benchmark Assessment • Benchmark 1

Benchmark 1

Vocabulary (continued)

6. What word means the opposite of possible?
   - Ⓐ likely
   - Ⓑ certain
   - Ⓒ predicted
   - Ⓓ heavy

7. Which word BEST completes both sentences?
   The _____ is in the drawer.
   You will need a _____ to sharpen that.
   - Ⓐ paper
   - Ⓑ knife
   - Ⓒ tool
   - ● file

8. Which word BEST completes both sentences?
   I came in _____ in the race.
   The light came on for about a _____.
   - Ⓐ last
   - Ⓑ minute
   - ● second
   - Ⓓ third

9. The big bed was cozy on a cold night. Cozy means
   - Ⓐ hard.
   - ● warm.
   - Ⓒ cold.
   - Ⓓ large.

10. Do not misplace your book or you will waste time looking for it. Misplace means
    - Ⓐ carry.
    - Ⓑ find.
    - Ⓒ read.
    - ● lose.

STOP

Benchmark Assessment • Benchmark 1   Level 4 • 11

Benchmark 1

Grammar, Usage, and Mechanics

Read each question. Fill in the bubble beside the answer in each group that is correct. If none of the answers is correct, choose the last answer, "none of the above."

1. Which sentence is written correctly?
   - Ⓐ Elizabeth is the name of the queen of england.
   - Ⓑ Elizabeth is the name of the Queen of England.
   - ● Elizabeth is the name of the queen of England.
   - Ⓓ none of the above

2. Which sentence is written incorrectly?
   - Ⓐ Balls, bats, and gloves are used to play baseball.
   - Ⓑ I had a sandwich, soup, and milk for lunch.
   - ● Stephen likes apples, bananas and oranges.
   - Ⓓ none of the above

3. Which sentence is written correctly?
   - Ⓐ Rob's favorite song is The Way We Were.
   - ● Rob's favorite song is "The Way We Were."
   - Ⓒ Rob's favorite song is, "The Way We Were."
   - Ⓓ none of the above

4. Which sentence is written incorrectly?
   - Ⓐ "It is beautiful!" Jose said.
   - ● "It's the end of the world the actor said."
   - Ⓒ Gerrald whispered, "I need some water."
   - Ⓓ none of the above

5. Which sentence is written correctly?
   - Ⓐ The horse ran around more happiest in the snow.
   - Ⓑ The horse ran around more happier in the snow.
   - Ⓒ The horse ran around most happy in the snow.
   - ● none of the above

GO ON ➡

12 • Level 4   Benchmark Assessment • Benchmark 1

Benchmark 1

Grammar, Usage, and Mechanics (continued)

6. Which sentence is written incorrectly?
   - ● Carl and Kwame runs to the store.
   - Ⓑ She travels to Europe and Africa.
   - Ⓒ Pizza and cookies are my favorite foods.
   - Ⓓ none of the above

7. Which sentence is written correctly?
   - Ⓐ I am going to buy me a fan.
   - ● I am going to buy myself a fan.
   - Ⓒ I am going to buy mine a fan.
   - Ⓓ none of the above

8. Which sentence is written correctly?
   - Ⓐ No one knew what to expect after the change is made.
   - ● No one knew what to expect after the change was made.
   - Ⓒ No one knows what to expect after the change will be made.
   - Ⓓ none of the above

9. Which sentence contains a compound predicate?
   - Ⓐ The tree growing in the pot is pretty.
   - ● A truck slowed down and turned into the parking lot.
   - Ⓒ The door to the basement has a broken lock.
   - Ⓓ none of the above

10. Which sentence contains a dependent clause?
    - ● I know what I am doing.
    - Ⓑ The customer asked for help from the clerk.
    - Ⓒ She left her jacket here, and Dan came back to get it.
    - Ⓓ none of the above

STOP

Benchmark Assessment • Benchmark 1   Level 4 • 13

Benchmark 1

Benchmark 1

Spelling

Read each group of words. Only one of the words is spelled correctly. Fill in the bubble under the word that is spelled correctly.

1. proven   provne   porven   provin
   (A)   (B)   (C)   (D)

2. bicicle   bicycle   bycicle   bisicle
   (A)   (B)   (C)   (D)

3. ratf   reft   rafte   raft
   (A)   (B)   (C)   (D)

4. laeder   leadre   leader   leeder
   (A)   (B)   (C)   (D)

5. fairle   fairly   fiarly   frialy
   (A)   (B)   (C)   (D)

Benchmark 1

Benchmark 1

Spelling (continued)

In each sentence, look for the underlined word that is spelled incorrectly. Focus on just the underlined word. Fill in the bubble next to the sentence with the misspelled word. If all the underlined words are spelled correctly, choose "correct as is."

6. (A) Meg wonderd if Pam were coming.
   (B) Perhaps Tim could help them fix it.
   (C) The maid cleaned the hotel room.
   (D) correct as is

7. (A) Zoo animals frighten my younger brother.
   (B) The man was on trial for his crime.
   (C) If we don't eat soon, I think I'll starve.
   (D) correct as is

8. (A) Scientists studied the unknown plant.
   (B) My mom takes her usaul walk around the block.
   (C) The explorers looked for the river's source.
   (D) correct as is

9. (A) The plumber must repair the pipes.
   (B) This land is flater than that land.
   (C) Jed has been working hard on his homework.
   (D) correct as is

10. (A) Paul is convinced that everyone will go.
    (B) The police observed the robber leaving.
    (C) Uncle Todd says Jon is his favorite nephew.
    (D) correct as is

STOP This is the end of the group-administered section of the Benchmark Assessment.

Benchmark 1

Benchmark 2 Answer Sheets

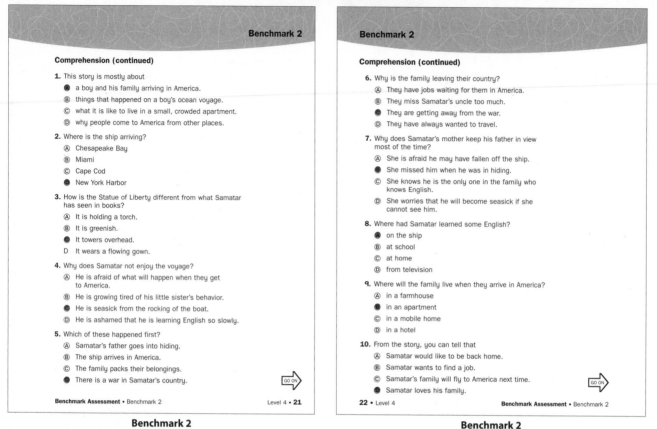

Comprehension (continued)

1. This story is mostly about
- Ⓐ a boy and his family arriving in America.
- Ⓑ things that happened on a boy's ocean voyage.
- Ⓒ what it is like to live in a small, crowded apartment.
- Ⓓ why people come to America from other places.

2. Where is the ship arriving?
- Ⓐ Chesapeake Bay
- Ⓑ Miami
- Ⓒ Cape Cod
- ⬤ New York Harbor

3. How is the Statue of Liberty different from what Samatar has seen in books?
- Ⓐ It is holding a torch.
- Ⓑ It is greenish.
- ⬤ It towers overhead.
- Ⓓ It wears a flowing gown.

4. Why does Samatar not enjoy the voyage?
- Ⓐ He is afraid of what will happen when they get to America.
- Ⓑ He is growing tired of his little sister's behavior.
- ⬤ He is seasick from the rocking of the boat.
- Ⓓ He is ashamed that he is learning English so slowly.

5. Which of these happened first?
- Ⓐ Samatar's father goes into hiding.
- Ⓑ The ship arrives in America.
- Ⓒ The family packs their belongings.
- ⬤ There is a war in Samatar's country.

Benchmark 2

Comprehension (continued)

6. Why is the family leaving their country?
- Ⓐ They have jobs waiting for them in America.
- Ⓑ They miss Samatar's uncle too much.
- ⬤ They are getting away from the war.
- Ⓓ They have always wanted to travel.

7. Why does Samatar's mother keep his father in view most of the time?
- Ⓐ She is afraid he may have fallen off the ship.
- ⬤ She missed him when he was in hiding.
- Ⓒ She knows he is the only one in the family who knows English.
- Ⓓ She worries that he will become seasick if she cannot see him.

8. Where had Samatar learned some English?
- ⬤ on the ship
- Ⓑ at school
- Ⓒ at home
- Ⓓ from television

9. Where will the family live when they arrive in America?
- Ⓐ in a farmhouse
- ⬤ in an apartment
- Ⓒ in a mobile home
- Ⓓ in a hotel

10. From the story, you can tell that
- Ⓐ Samatar would like to be back home.
- Ⓑ Samatar wants to find a job.
- Ⓒ Samatar's family will fly to America next time.
- ⬤ Samatar loves his family.

Benchmark 2

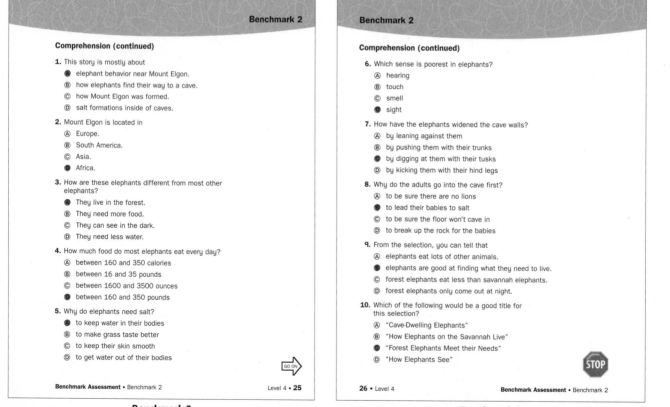

Comprehension (continued)

1. This story is mostly about
- ⬤ elephant behavior near Mount Elgon.
- Ⓑ how elephants find their way to a cave.
- Ⓒ how Mount Elgon was formed.
- Ⓓ salt formations inside of caves.

2. Mount Elgon is located in
- Ⓐ Europe.
- Ⓑ South America.
- Ⓒ Asia.
- ⬤ Africa.

3. How are these elephants different from most other elephants?
- ⬤ They live in the forest.
- Ⓑ They need more food.
- Ⓒ They can see in the dark.
- Ⓓ They need less water.

4. How much food do most elephants eat every day?
- Ⓐ between 160 and 350 calories
- Ⓑ between 16 and 35 pounds
- Ⓒ between 1600 and 3500 ounces
- ⬤ between 160 and 350 pounds

5. Why do elephants need salt?
- ⬤ to keep water in their bodies
- Ⓑ to make grass taste better
- Ⓒ to keep their skin smooth
- Ⓓ to get water out of their bodies

Benchmark 2

Comprehension (continued)

6. Which sense is poorest in elephants?
- Ⓐ hearing
- Ⓑ touch
- Ⓒ smell
- ⬤ sight

7. How have the elephants widened the cave walls?
- Ⓐ by leaning against them
- Ⓑ by pushing them with their trunks
- ⬤ by digging at them with their tusks
- Ⓓ by kicking them with their hind legs

8. Why do the adults go into the cave first?
- Ⓐ to be sure there are no lions
- ⬤ to lead their babies to salt
- Ⓒ to be sure the floor won't cave in
- Ⓓ to break up the rock for the babies

9. From the selection, you can tell that
- Ⓐ elephants eat lots of other animals.
- ⬤ elephants are good at finding what they need to live.
- Ⓒ forest elephants eat less than savannah elephants.
- Ⓓ forest elephants only come out at night.

10. Which of the following would be a good title for this selection?
- Ⓐ "Cave-Dwelling Elephants"
- Ⓑ "How Elephants on the Savannah Live"
- ⬤ "Forest Elephants Meet their Needs"
- Ⓓ "How Elephants See"

Benchmark 2

Benchmark Assessment • Benchmark 2

Vocabulary

Read each item. Fill in the bubble for the answer you think is correct.

1. Briefly means
   - Ⓐ for a short time.
   - Ⓑ friendly.
   - Ⓒ without looking.
   - Ⓓ cleanly.

2. Disturb is the base word in disturbing. Disturbing means
   - Ⓐ respecting.
   - Ⓑ traveling.
   - Ⓒ troubling.
   - Ⓓ laughing.

3. Biology means
   - Ⓐ the study of space.
   - Ⓑ the study of history.
   - Ⓒ the study of rocks.
   - Ⓓ the study of living things.

4. What word means about the same as anxious?
   - Ⓐ happy
   - Ⓑ calm
   - Ⓒ nervous
   - Ⓓ twisted

5. What word means about the same as vanish?
   - Ⓐ jump
   - Ⓑ disappear
   - Ⓒ walk
   - Ⓓ arrive

GO ON

Benchmark 2

Vocabulary (continued)

6. What word means the opposite of enormous?
   - Ⓐ old
   - Ⓒ huge
   - Ⓑ ugly
   - Ⓓ tiny

7. Which word BEST completes both sentences?
   My dog _____ when it gets too hot.
   These are my new _____.
   - Ⓐ pants
   - Ⓒ hides
   - Ⓑ shorts
   - Ⓓ shoes

8. Which word BEST completes both sentences?
   We heard a great _____ last night.
   A metal _____ went around the tree.
   - Ⓐ record
   - Ⓒ band
   - Ⓑ concert
   - Ⓓ strap

9. A foul odor came from the swamp. Odor means
   - Ⓐ animal.
   - Ⓒ taste.
   - Ⓑ bug.
   - Ⓓ smell.

10. The old horse was very gentle with children. Gentle means
    - Ⓐ calm.
    - Ⓒ fast.
    - Ⓑ nervous.
    - Ⓓ bored.

STOP

Benchmark 2

Grammar, Usage, and Mechanics

Read each question. Fill in the bubble beside the answer in each group that is correct. If none of the answers is correct, choose the last answer, "none of the above."

1. Which sentence is written correctly?
   - Ⓐ We went to Salt Lake City for Thanksgiving.
   - Ⓑ We went to Salt Lake city for Thanksgiving.
   - Ⓒ We went to Salt Lake City for thanksgiving.
   - Ⓓ none of the above

2. Which sentence is written incorrectly?
   - Ⓐ Here is what I brought: pop, candy, and videos.
   - Ⓑ These are examples of citrus fruit: Oranges, grapefruit, lemons, and limes.
   - Ⓒ You must choose your favorite color: pink, purple, blue, or green.
   - Ⓓ none of the above

3. Which sentence is written correctly?
   - Ⓐ Homer is supposed to have written The Odyssey.
   - Ⓑ Homer is supposed to have written the Odyssey.
   - Ⓒ Homer is supposed to have written "the odyssey."
   - Ⓓ none of the above

4. Which sentence is written incorrectly?
   - Ⓐ "Spare me!" shouted the prisoner.
   - Ⓒ Sue said "We will try again later."
   - Ⓑ "I do not like mushrooms," said Bobby.
   - Ⓓ none of the above

5. Which sentence is written correctly?
   - Ⓐ Ben's happiest memories are of the time he spent in school.
   - Ⓑ Ben's most happiest memories are of the time he spent in school.
   - Ⓒ Ben's most happier memories are of the time he spent in school.
   - Ⓓ none of the above

GO ON

Benchmark 2

Grammar, Usage, and Mechanics (continued)

6. Which sentence is written correctly?
   - Ⓐ Frank or Ella know the answer.
   - Ⓑ Frank and Ella knows the answer.
   - Ⓒ Frank or Ella knows the answer.
   - Ⓓ none of the above

7. Which sentence is written correctly?
   - Ⓐ He is carrying a bag in they hand.
   - Ⓑ He is carrying a bag in him hand.
   - Ⓒ He is carrying a bag in their hand.
   - Ⓓ none of the above

8. Which sentence is written incorrectly?
   - Ⓐ Though he tried hard, Julio's team lost.
   - Ⓑ When we go out to eat, Sheila does not eat much.
   - Ⓒ Aaron fixes dinner even though he was not hungry.
   - Ⓓ none of the above

9. Which sentence contains a compound predicate?
   - Ⓐ A cow and a goat wandered down the trail.
   - Ⓑ It took four days to finish the job.
   - Ⓒ The puppy stopped and smelled the flower.
   - Ⓓ none of the above

10. Which sentence contains a dependent clause?
    - Ⓐ Mrs. Hart wants to write a play about her family.
    - Ⓑ She carries a pack on her back and a book under her arm.
    - Ⓒ You will sleep if you drink warm milk.
    - Ⓓ none of the above

STOP

Benchmark 2

Benchmark 2 Answer Sheets

Spelling

Read each group of words. Only one of the words is spelled correctly. Fill in the bubble under the word that is spelled correctly.

1. staroge Ⓐ | storage ● | stroage Ⓒ | storaje Ⓓ
2. degre Ⓐ | deegre Ⓑ | dergree Ⓒ | degree ●
3. jogging ● | joging Ⓑ | jogginng Ⓒ | joggin Ⓓ
4. fatsen Ⓐ | fastin Ⓑ | fasten ● | festen Ⓓ
5. lawen Ⓐ | lawne Ⓑ | lanw Ⓒ | lawn ●

Benchmark 2

Spelling (continued)

In each sentence, look for the underlined word that is spelled incorrectly. Focus on just the underlined word. Fill in the bubble next to the sentence with the misspelled word. If all the underlined words are spelled correctly, choose "correct as is."

6. ● The casheir gave us the wrong change.
   Ⓑ Monday is laundry day at our house.
   Ⓒ Sometimes Leah is impatient with her little brother.
   Ⓓ correct as is

7. Ⓐ Avery learned a new chord on his guitar.
   Ⓑ The queen chose a jewel for her crown.
   ● The hikers found pieces of pertrified wood.
   Ⓓ correct as is

8. Ⓐ Liam needed his parents' approval to join the team.
   Ⓑ My little sister can be a real nuisance!
   ● Semir's brother is a junour in high school.
   Ⓓ correct as is

9. Ⓐ At the pool, Pedro likes to plunge right into the water.
   ● The friends made up after their quarrell.
   Ⓒ The hotel provides breakfast every morning.
   Ⓓ correct as is

10. Ⓐ The builder gave us an estimate for our new house.
    Ⓑ Visitors need a passport to cross the border.
    Ⓒ Do you have something to occupy yourself while you wait?
    ● correct as is

STOP This is the end of the group-administered section of the Benchmark Assessment.

Benchmark 2

Benchmark 3 Answer Sheets

Comprehension (continued)

1. This story is mostly about
   - Ⓐ a girl learning to tie a headscarf.
   - Ⓑ what it is like to be in the hospital.
   - ● a girl's recovery from cancer.
   - Ⓓ how hard it is to be in middle school.

2. Why has Angel missed so much school?
   - ● She has been sick.
   - Ⓑ She is new in town.
   - Ⓒ She is very smart.
   - Ⓓ She has few friends.

3. Why does Angel think her friends have forgotten her?
   - Ⓐ She does not get cards from them any more.
   - ● They do not come to visit her as much.
   - Ⓒ They do not recognize her without hair.
   - Ⓓ She does not see them when she arrives at school.

4. On her first day of school, Angel's hair is like
   - Ⓐ silk.
   - Ⓑ steel wool.
   - Ⓒ banana peel.
   - ● peach fuzz.

5. How does Angel get to school on her first day back?
   - Ⓐ Dara walks with her.
   - ● Her dad drives her.
   - Ⓒ She takes the bus.
   - D She rides her bike.

Benchmark 3

Comprehension (continued)

6. Who comes to Angel as she arrives at school?
   - Ⓐ the principal
   - ● her friend Dara
   - Ⓒ the school nurse
   - Ⓓ her dad

7. Why are the other students wearing scarves?
   - ● to help Angel feel better
   - Ⓑ to be part of the newest fashion
   - Ⓒ to practice tying headscarves
   - Ⓓ to show school spirit

8. Dara helps Angel in all of these ways EXCEPT
   - Ⓐ teaching her to tie a headscarf.
   - Ⓑ skipping homeroom to find her first class.
   - ● helping her with math homework.
   - Ⓓ getting the other students to wear scarves.

9. A word you could use to describe Dara is
   - Ⓐ funny.
   - Ⓑ energetic.
   - Ⓒ athletic.
   - ● kind.

10. From this story, you know that
   - Ⓐ Angel is completely cured of cancer.
   - Ⓑ Dara is an excellent student.
   - ● Angel has many friends at school.
   - Ⓓ Angel's teachers help her catch up.

Benchmark 3

Comprehension (continued)

1. This story is mostly about
   - Ⓐ how a parachute works.
   - Ⓑ how to save money on a parachute.
   - Ⓒ what skydiving feels like.
   - ● an unusual activity.

2. The S in BASE stands for
   - Ⓐ silk.
   - ● span.
   - Ⓒ space.
   - Ⓓ sky.

3. A canyon would be an example of
   - Ⓐ Building.
   - Ⓑ Antenna.
   - Ⓒ Span.
   - ● Earth.

4. BASE jumpers are concerned about all of these problems EXCEPT
   - ● having to pay a lot for fuel.
   - Ⓑ finding a safe place to jump.
   - Ⓒ getting permission to jump.
   - Ⓓ making sure their chutes work.

5. How are BASE jumpers like skydivers?
   - Ⓐ Both are in freefall when they jump.
   - Ⓑ Neither requires a lot of space to jump.
   - ● Both jumpers need parachutes
   - Ⓓ Neither costs very much money.

Benchmark 3

Comprehension (continued)

6. Why do BASE jumpers chutes open more quickly than a skydiver's?
   - Ⓐ The BASE jumper's chute is made of different material.
   - Ⓑ The BASE jumper is falling more quickly than the skydiver.
   - ● The BASE jumper is closer to the ground than the skydiver.
   - Ⓓ The BASE jumper's chute is much larger than the skydiver's.

7. Which of these would be a good choice for BASE jumping?
   - Ⓐ the antenna for the radio station across town
   - ● a tall cliff with a meadow below it
   - Ⓒ a 40-story apartment building in the city
   - Ⓓ in the middle of a ranch in Texas

8. Property owners do not want BASE jumpers on their property mostly because
   - Ⓐ the jumpers do not have any money.
   - Ⓑ the owners do not like jumpers.
   - Ⓒ the property will be damaged.
   - ● the jumpers might get hurt.

9. Which of these is not a reason you need lots of space for your landing area?
   - Ⓐ so you will not hit anything when you land
   - ● so the airplane has enough room to land
   - Ⓒ so other people can watch you jump
   - Ⓓ so you will not damage your chute when you land

10. BASE jumpers are probably people who
   - Ⓐ make friends easily.
   - ● like taking risks.
   - Ⓑ enjoy going to the movies.
   - Ⓓ studied hard in school.

STOP

Benchmark 3

Benchmark 3 Answer Sheets

Vocabulary

Read each item. Fill in the bubble for the answer you think is correct.

1. Dislike means
   - Ⓐ sing.
   - 🅑 hate.
   - Ⓒ love.
   - Ⓓ trust.

2. Life is the base word in lifeless. Lifeless means
   - Ⓐ alive.
   - Ⓑ young.
   - 🅒 dead.
   - Ⓓ kind.

3. Democracy means
   - Ⓐ government by voting.
   - Ⓑ many people in one place.
   - Ⓒ walking to a distant place.
   - Ⓓ finding something by accident.

4. What word means about the same as muttered?
   - Ⓐ shouted
   - Ⓑ whispered
   - Ⓒ cried
   - 🅓 mumbled

5. What word means about the same as contented?
   - 🅐 satisfied
   - Ⓑ annoyed
   - Ⓒ angry
   - Ⓓ confused

GO ON

Benchmark 3

Vocabulary (continued)

6. What word means the opposite of exciting?
   - Ⓐ new
   - 🅑 dull
   - Ⓒ silly
   - Ⓓ long

7. Which word BEST completes both sentences?
   My mother will ____ the walls.
   Is this today's ____?
   - Ⓐ paint
   - Ⓒ repair
   - 🅑 paper
   - Ⓓ mail

8. Which word BEST completes both sentences?
   Mr. Rose paid a parking ____.
   The worker did a ____ job.
   - Ⓐ fee
   - 🅒 fine
   - Ⓑ great
   - Ⓓ good

9. Be sure to get your parents' approval for the trip. Approval means
   - Ⓐ address.
   - Ⓒ packages.
   - 🅑 permission.
   - Ⓓ names.

10. We received an appeal for donations. Appeal means
   - 🅐 request
   - Ⓒ notice.
   - Ⓑ ticket.
   - Ⓓ demand.

STOP

Benchmark 3

Grammar, Usage, and Mechanics

Read each question. Fill in the bubble beside the answer in each group that is correct. If none of the answers is correct, choose the last answer, "none of the above."

1. Which sentence is written correctly?
   - Ⓐ She attends Four Corners school on Federal Street.
   - Ⓑ She attends Four Corners school on Federal street.
   - Ⓒ She attends four Corners School on Federal Street.
   - 🅓 none of the above

2. Which sentence is written incorrectly?
   - 🅐 There are three primary colors, red, yellow, and blue.
   - Ⓑ There are two things I always carry: a comb and ten dollars.
   - Ⓒ She only likes three people: her aunt, her mom, and her dad.
   - Ⓓ none of the above

3. Which sentence is written correctly?
   - Ⓐ The Wizard of Oz will only be showing for a week.
   - Ⓑ "The wizard of oz" will only be showing for a week.
   - Ⓒ The wizard of oz will only be showing for a week.
   - 🅓 none of the above

4. Which sentence is written correctly?
   - 🅐 "We have to go home now," Mother said.
   - Ⓑ We have to go home now Mother said.
   - Ⓒ "We have to go home now, Mother said."
   - Ⓓ none of the above

5. Which sentence is written correctly?
   - 🅐 The brown cow lazily chewed its food.
   - Ⓑ The brown cow lazy chewed its food.
   - Ⓒ The brown cow lazier chewed its food.
   - Ⓓ none of the above

GO ON

Benchmark 3

Grammar, Usage, and Mechanics (continued)

6. Which sentence is written incorrectly?
   - Ⓐ Was it Ted or Tommy who saw it?
   - 🅑 A parent or teacher am coming with us.
   - Ⓒ My mom or my dad took out the trash.
   - Ⓓ none of the above

7. Which sentence is written correctly?
   - 🅐 My sister and I both like sardines.
   - Ⓑ My sister and me both like sardines.
   - Ⓒ My sister and him both like sardines.
   - Ⓓ none of the above

8. Which sentence is written incorrectly?
   - 🅐 The cat catches the mouse as it left its hole.
   - Ⓑ Johnny was hit hard in yesterday's game.
   - Ⓒ Amber loves to play outside when the snow falls.
   - Ⓓ none of the above

9. Which sentence contains a compound subject?
   - Ⓐ Everyone wore costumes to school for the play.
   - Ⓑ The neighbors bought a new lawnmower and a new rake.
   - 🅒 Ducks and geese spend the winter at the lake.
   - Ⓓ none of the above

10. Which sentence contains a dependent clause?
   - Ⓐ The bus went to the next town but Jerry stayed at home.
   - Ⓑ The butterfly was caught by a spider.
   - 🅒 Runners eat pretzels when they need salt.
   - Ⓓ none of the above

STOP

Benchmark 3

Benchmark 3 Answer Sheets

Spelling

Read each group of words. Only one of the words is spelled correctly. Fill in the bubble under the word that is spelled correctly.

1. portest Ⓐ protset Ⓑ protest ● pretost Ⓓ

2. stareo Ⓐ steroe Ⓑ sterrio Ⓒ stereo ●

3. equally ● eqaully Ⓑ equaly Ⓒ equilly Ⓓ

4. pulbic Ⓐ public ● poblic Ⓒ publick Ⓓ

5. main ● mian Ⓑ moin Ⓒ naim Ⓓ

GO ON →

Benchmark Assessment • Benchmark 3   Level 4 • 47

Benchmark 3

Spelling (continued)

In each sentence, look for the underlined word that is spelled incorrectly. Focus on just the underlined word. Fill in the bubble next to the sentence with the misspelled word. If all the underlined words are spelled correctly, choose "correct as is."

6. Ⓐ Dad gave Mom a <u>diamond</u> ring.
   Ⓑ Paula's parents <u>rent</u> that house.
   ● Humans <u>braethe</u> air to stay alive.
   Ⓓ correct as is

7. Ⓐ Do you <u>agree</u> with his answer?
   Ⓑ We stood in a <u>shelter</u> during the storm.
   Ⓒ Look both ways before you step off the <u>curb</u>.
   ● correct as is

8. Ⓐ Try to <u>avoid</u> the icy patches.
   Ⓑ This <u>level</u> of the mall has a food court.
   ● The police solved the <u>mistery</u>.
   Ⓓ correct as is

9. Ⓐ A cheetah is a <u>rapid</u> runner.
   ● Nancy can put this <u>puzzel</u> together.
   Ⓒ The sign said, "Do not <u>disturb</u>."
   Ⓓ correct as is

10. ● The explorers found a <u>pasage</u> through the mountains.
    Ⓑ One problem for the poor in many places is <u>hunger</u>.
    Ⓒ The farmers found <u>plentiful</u> water in the valley.
    Ⓓ correct as is

STOP This is the end of the group-administered section of the Benchmark Assessment.

48 • Level 4   Benchmark Assessment • Benchmark 3

Benchmark 3

Benchmark 4 Answer Sheets

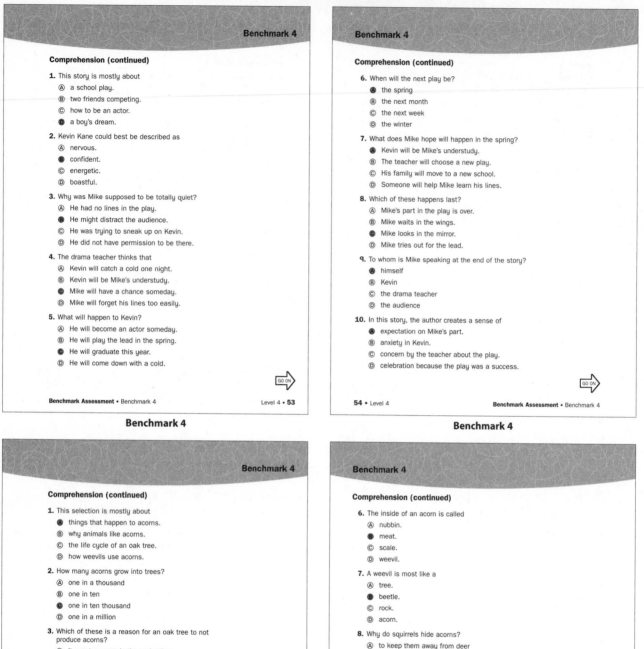

Comprehension (continued)

1. This story is mostly about
 Ⓐ a school play.
 Ⓑ two friends competing.
 Ⓒ how to be an actor.
 ● a boy's dream.

2. Kevin Kane could best be described as
 Ⓐ nervous.
 ● confident.
 Ⓒ energetic.
 Ⓓ boastful.

3. Why was Mike supposed to be totally quiet?
 Ⓐ He had no lines in the play.
 ● He might distract the audience.
 Ⓒ He was trying to sneak up on Kevin.
 Ⓓ He did not have permission to be there.

4. The drama teacher thinks that
 Ⓐ Kevin will catch a cold one night.
 Ⓑ Kevin will be Mike's understudy.
 ● Mike will have a chance someday.
 Ⓓ Mike will forget his lines too easily.

5. What will happen to Kevin?
 Ⓐ He will become an actor someday.
 Ⓑ He will play the lead in the spring.
 ● He will graduate this year.
 Ⓓ He will come down with a cold.

GO ON

Benchmark Assessment • Benchmark 4

Level 4 • **53**

Benchmark 4

Comprehension (continued)

6. When will the next play be?
 ● the spring
 Ⓑ the next month
 Ⓒ the next week
 Ⓓ the winter

7. What does Mike hope will happen in the spring?
 Ⓐ Kevin will be Mike's understudy.
 Ⓑ The teacher will choose a new play.
 Ⓒ His family will move to a new school.
 Ⓓ Someone will help Mike learn his lines.

8. Which of these happens last?
 Ⓐ Mike's part in the play is over.
 Ⓑ Mike waits in the wings.
 ● Mike looks in the mirror.
 Ⓓ Mike tries out for the lead.

9. To whom is Mike speaking at the end of the story?
 ● himself
 Ⓑ Kevin
 Ⓒ the drama teacher
 Ⓓ the audience

10. In this story, the author creates a sense of
 ● expectation on Mike's part.
 Ⓑ anxiety in Kevin.
 Ⓒ concern by the teacher about the play.
 Ⓓ celebration because the play was a success.

GO ON

54 • Level 4

Benchmark Assessment • Benchmark 4

Benchmark 4

Comprehension (continued)

1. This selection is mostly about
 ● things that happen to acorns.
 Ⓑ why animals like acorns.
 Ⓒ the life cycle of an oak tree.
 Ⓓ how weevils use acorns.

2. How many acorns grow into trees?
 Ⓐ one in a thousand
 Ⓑ one in ten
 ● one in ten thousand
 Ⓓ one in a million

3. Which of these is a reason for an oak tree to not produce acorns?
 Ⓐ It was too warm in the springtime.
 Ⓑ There was too much rain.
 Ⓒ The tree got too much sun.
 ● The tree is not old enough.

4. From this selection, you know that oak trees have
 Ⓐ wood that is hard to cut.
 Ⓑ leaves that stay green all year.
 ● tiny flowers.
 Ⓓ weak roots.

5. Which of these happens first?
 Ⓐ A young weevil cuts a hole in the acorn.
 Ⓑ An adult weevil lays an egg in a hole.
 ● An adult weevil drills a hole in the acorn.
 Ⓓ A young weevil eats the meat from an acorn.

GO ON

Benchmark Assessment • Benchmark 4

Level 4 • **57**

Benchmark 4

Comprehension (continued)

6. The inside of an acorn is called
 Ⓐ nubbin.
 ● meat.
 Ⓒ scale.
 Ⓓ weevil.

7. A weevil is most like a
 Ⓐ tree.
 ● beetle.
 Ⓒ rock.
 Ⓓ acorn.

8. Why do squirrels hide acorns?
 Ⓐ to keep them away from deer
 Ⓑ to grow new oak trees
 ● to eat during the winter
 Ⓓ to give weevils a place for eggs

9. The selection says there was a very old oak tree in
 ● Maryland.
 Ⓑ New York.
 Ⓒ Florida.
 Ⓓ Michigan.

10. From the selection, you know that
 Ⓐ acorns are a squirrel's favorite food.
 Ⓑ most acorns are eaten by young weevils.
 Ⓒ deer like to eat small oak trees.
 ● some oak trees are older than people.

STOP

58 • Level 4

Benchmark Assessment • Benchmark 4

Benchmark 4

Benchmark Assessment • Benchmark 4

Benchmark 4 Answer Sheets

Vocabulary

Read each item. Fill in the bubble for the answer you think is correct.

1. <u>Scientist</u> means
   - (A) a school that teaches science.
   - (B) a building where people study science.
   - (C) a project that uses science.
   - ● a person who studies science.

2. <u>Appear</u> is the base word in <u>disappear</u>. <u>Disappear</u> means
   - (A) equal.
   - ● vanish.
   - (C) control.
   - (D) defend.

3. <u>Native</u> means
   - (A) a boat with sails.
   - (B) a forest in a warm place.
   - ● a person from a place.
   - (D) a city from long ago.

4. What word means about the same as <u>rim</u>?
   - (A) center
   - (B) entry
   - ● edge
   - (D) bottom

5. What word means about the same as <u>locate</u>?
   - (A) lose
   - ● find
   - (C) acquire
   - (D) damage

GO ON

Benchmark Assessment • Benchmark 4   Level 4 • **59**

Benchmark 4

Vocabulary (continued)

6. What word means the opposite of <u>distant</u>?
   - ● nearby
   - (B) far away
   - (C) tall
   - (D) tree-covered

7. Which word BEST completes both sentences?
   The _____ is still in the can of paint.
   The deer walked through the _____.
   - (A) can   (C) woods
   - ● brush   (D) jar

8. Which word BEST completes both sentences?
   We looked in both _____.
   What do the _____ say?
   - (A) paths   (C) words
   - ● directions   (D) boxes

9. Kim cannot find anything in her <u>untidy</u> room.
   <u>Untidy</u> means
   - (A) large.   ● messy.
   - (B) clean.   (D) dark.

10. Each <u>nation</u> sent a team to the Olympics.
    <u>Nation</u> means
    - (A) town.   (C) city.
    - ● country.   (D) state.

STOP

60 • Level 4   Benchmark Assessment • Benchmark 4

Benchmark 4

Grammar, Usage, and Mechanics

Read each question. Fill in the bubble beside the answer in each group that is correct. If none of the answers is correct, choose the last answer, "none of the above."

1. Which sentence is written <u>incorrectly</u>?
   - (A) Brian was also known as Wonder Boy.
   - ● They speak Japanese at Home and English at School.
   - (C) Orlando, Florida is the home of Disney World.
   - (D) none of the above

2. Which sentence is written correctly?
   - (A) Bring these on the hike water, a snack, and sunscreen.
   - (B) Bring these on the hike: Water, a snack, and sunscreen.
   - ● Bring these on the hike: water, a snack, and sunscreen.
   - (D) none of the above

3. Which sentence is written correctly?
   - ● There is always a copy of the magazine <u>Smithsonian</u> at our house.
   - (B) There is always a copy of the magazine smithsonian at our house.
   - (C) There is always a copy of the "magazine Smithsonian" at our house.
   - (D) none of the above

4. Which sentence is written correctly?
   - (A) "I want to ride the roller coaster again" shouted Lynn!
   - ● "I want to ride the roller coaster again!" shouted Lynn.
   - (C) "I want to ride the roller coaster again"! shouted Lynn.
   - (D) none of the above

5. Which sentence is written <u>incorrectly</u>?
   - (A) My tallest friend reached up to the top shelf.
   - ● Louise tied the laces on her shoe more tighter.
   - (C) Juanita is the friendliest person I know.
   - (D) none of the above

GO ON

Benchmark Assessment • Benchmark 4   Level 4 • **61**

Benchmark 4

Grammar, Usage, and Mechanics (continued)

6. Which sentence is written correctly?
   - (A) She and I is the players the team wanted.
   - (B) She and I was the players the team wanted.
   - ● She and I were the players the team wanted.
   - (D) none of the above

7. Which sentence is written correctly?
   - (A) You are going to make that men laugh.
   - (B) You are going to make those man laugh.
   - ● You are going to make that man laugh.
   - (D) none of the above

8. Which sentence is written correctly?
   - (A) Nadia does not get discouraged when the work was difficult.
   - ● Nadia does not get discouraged when the work is difficult.
   - (C) Nadia did not get discouraged when the work is difficult.
   - (D) none of the above

9. Which sentence contains a compound subject?
   - ● Cactus and large rocks were placed around the garden.
   - (B) The phone doesn't seem to be working.
   - (C) A strange bird came to the feeder yesterday afternoon.
   - (D) none of the above

10. Which sentence contains a dependent clause?
    - (A) Digging ditches is hard work.
    - (B) The team wanted to win, so the coach had extra practice.
    - (C) Danny painted a picture of a mountain scene.
    - ● none of the above

STOP

62 • Level 4   Benchmark Assessment • Benchmark 4

Benchmark 4

Benchmark 4 Answer Sheets

Spelling

Read each group of words. Only one of the words is spelled correctly. Fill in the bubble under the word that is spelled correctly.

1. macking Ⓐ   makin Ⓑ   makking Ⓒ   making ●

2. chilly ●   chily Ⓑ   chilley Ⓒ   chelliy Ⓓ

3. corwd Ⓐ   croud Ⓑ   crowd ●   crowt Ⓓ

4. barfoot Ⓐ   barefoot ●   barefot Ⓒ   bairfoot Ⓓ

5. scarecly Ⓐ   sarcely Ⓑ   scaircely Ⓒ   scarcely ●

GO ON →

Spelling (continued)

In each sentence, look for the underlined word that is spelled incorrectly. Focus on just the underlined word. Fill in the bubble next to the sentence with the misspelled word. If all the underlined words are spelled correctly, choose "correct as is."

6. ● The teacher wrote on the chaklboard.
   Ⓑ My friend goes to the academy of dance.
   Ⓒ The subway is the fastest way into town.
   Ⓓ correct as is

7. Ⓐ What happens next?
   ● We see an ocasional movie.
   Ⓒ Pete needs film for his camera.
   Ⓓ correct as is

8. ● The dog had flease.
   Ⓑ Give her a little poke to wake her up.
   Ⓒ My cat's paws were all muddy.
   Ⓓ correct as is

9. Ⓐ Sandy needs a boost to climb the tree.
   Ⓑ The police offered a reward for clues.
   Ⓒ Aunt Nell returns on the noon train.
   ● correct as is

10. Ⓐ Fill this bucket with water.
    Ⓑ The police helped the lost boy.
    ● You will remian here until we get back.
    Ⓓ correct as is

STOP This is the end of the group-administered section of the Benchmark Assessment.

Benchmark 4

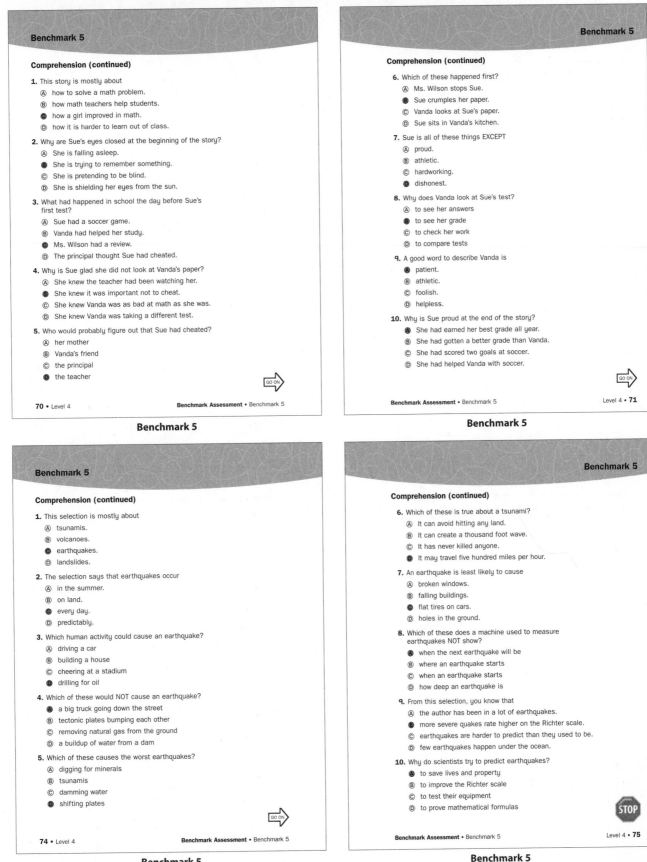

Benchmark 5

Comprehension (continued)

1. This story is mostly about
(A) how to solve a math problem.
(B) how math teachers help students.
(C) how a girl improved in math.
(D) how it is harder to learn out of class.

2. Why are Sue's eyes closed at the beginning of the story?
(A) She is falling asleep.
(B) She is trying to remember something.
(C) She is pretending to be blind.
(D) She is shielding her eyes from the sun.

3. What had happened in school the day before Sue's first test?
(A) Sue had a soccer game.
(B) Vanda had helped her study.
(C) Ms. Wilson had a review.
(D) The principal thought Sue had cheated.

4. Why is Sue glad she did not look at Vanda's paper?
(A) She knew the teacher had been watching her.
(B) She knew it was important not to cheat.
(C) She knew Vanda was as bad at math as she was.
(D) She knew Vanda was taking a different test.

5. Who would probably figure out that Sue had cheated?
(A) her mother
(B) Vanda's friend
(C) the principal
(D) the teacher

GO ON

70 • Level 4   Benchmark Assessment • Benchmark 5

Benchmark 5

Benchmark 5

Comprehension (continued)

6. Which of these happened first?
(A) Ms. Wilson stops Sue.
(B) Sue crumples her paper.
(C) Vanda looks at Sue's paper.
(D) Sue sits in Vanda's kitchen.

7. Sue is all of these things EXCEPT
(A) proud.
(B) athletic.
(C) hardworking.
(D) dishonest.

8. Why does Vanda look at Sue's test?
(A) to see her answers
(B) to see her grade
(C) to check her work
(D) to compare tests

9. A good word to describe Vanda is
(A) patient.
(B) athletic.
(C) foolish.
(D) helpless.

10. Why is Sue proud at the end of the story?
(A) She had earned her best grade all year.
(B) She had gotten a better grade than Vanda.
(C) She had scored two goals at soccer.
(D) She had helped Vanda with soccer.

GO ON

Benchmark Assessment • Benchmark 5   Level 4 • 71

Benchmark 5

Benchmark 5

Comprehension (continued)

1. This selection is mostly about
(A) tsunamis.
(B) volcanoes.
(C) earthquakes.
(D) landslides.

2. The selection says that earthquakes occur
(A) in the summer.
(B) on land.
(C) every day.
(D) predictably.

3. Which human activity could cause an earthquake?
(A) driving a car
(B) building a house
(C) cheering at a stadium
(D) drilling for oil

4. Which of these would NOT cause an earthquake?
(A) a big truck going down the street
(B) tectonic plates bumping each other
(C) removing natural gas from the ground
(D) a buildup of water from a dam

5. Which of these causes the worst earthquakes?
(A) digging for minerals
(B) tsunamis
(C) damming water
(D) shifting plates

GO ON

74 • Level 4   Benchmark Assessment • Benchmark 5

Benchmark 5

Benchmark 5

Comprehension (continued)

6. Which of these is true about a tsunami?
(A) It can avoid hitting any land.
(B) It can create a thousand foot wave.
(C) It has never killed anyone.
(D) It may travel five hundred miles per hour.

7. An earthquake is least likely to cause
(A) broken windows.
(B) falling buildings.
(C) flat tires on cars.
(D) holes in the ground.

8. Which of these does a machine used to measure earthquakes NOT show?
(A) when the next earthquake will be
(B) where an earthquake starts
(C) when an earthquake starts
(D) how deep an earthquake is

9. From this selection, you know that
(A) the author has been in a lot of earthquakes.
(B) more severe quakes rate higher on the Richter scale.
(C) earthquakes are harder to predict than they used to be.
(D) few earthquakes happen under the ocean.

10. Why do scientists try to predict earthquakes?
(A) to save lives and property
(B) to improve the Richter scale
(C) to test their equipment
(D) to prove mathematical formulas

STOP

Benchmark Assessment • Benchmark 5   Level 4 • 75

Benchmark 5

Benchmark 5 Answer Sheets

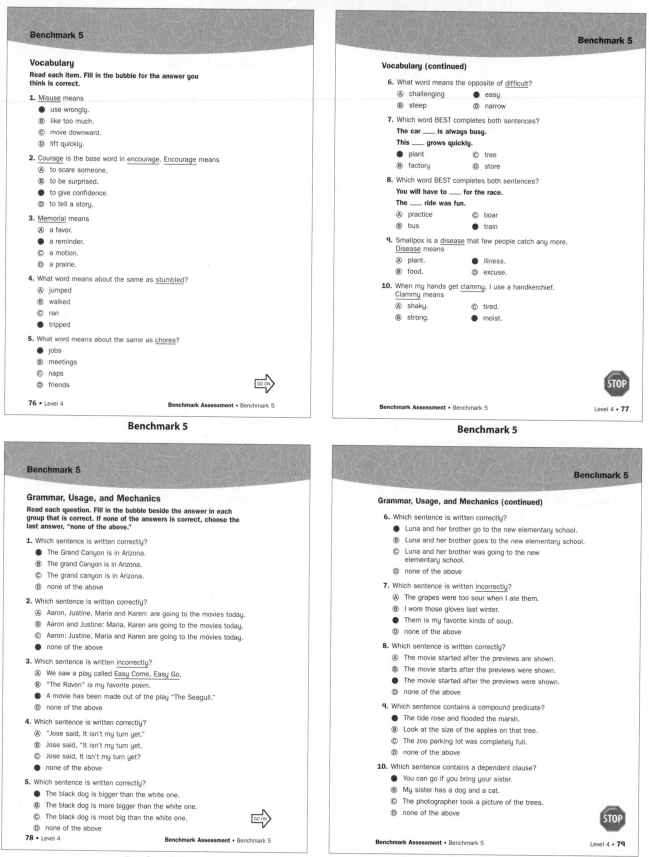

Benchmark 5

Vocabulary

Read each item. Fill in the bubble for the answer you think is correct.

1. <u>Misuse</u> means
   - ● use wrongly.
   - Ⓑ like too much.
   - Ⓒ move downward.
   - Ⓓ lift quickly.

2. <u>Courage</u> is the base word in <u>encourage</u>. <u>Encourage</u> means
   - Ⓐ to scare someone.
   - Ⓑ to be surprised.
   - ● to give confidence.
   - Ⓓ to tell a story.

3. <u>Memorial</u> means
   - Ⓐ a favor.
   - ● a reminder.
   - Ⓒ a motion.
   - Ⓓ a prairie.

4. What word means about the same as <u>stumbled</u>?
   - Ⓐ jumped
   - Ⓑ walked
   - Ⓒ ran
   - ● tripped

5. What word means about the same as <u>chores</u>?
   - ● jobs
   - Ⓑ meetings
   - Ⓒ naps
   - Ⓓ friends

Benchmark 5

Benchmark 5

Vocabulary (continued)

6. What word means the opposite of <u>difficult</u>?
   - Ⓐ challenging
   - ● easy
   - Ⓑ steep
   - Ⓓ narrow

7. Which word BEST completes both sentences?

   The car ___ is always busy.

   This ___ grows quickly.
   - ● plant
   - Ⓒ tree
   - Ⓑ factory
   - Ⓓ store

8. Which word BEST completes both sentences?

   You will have to ___ for the race.

   The ___ ride was fun.
   - Ⓐ practice
   - Ⓒ boar
   - Ⓑ bus
   - ● train

9. Smallpox is a <u>disease</u> that few people catch any more. <u>Disease</u> means
   - Ⓐ plant.
   - ● illness.
   - Ⓑ food.
   - Ⓓ excuse.

10. When my hands get <u>clammy</u>, I use a handkerchief. <u>Clammy</u> means
    - Ⓐ shaky.
    - Ⓒ tired.
    - Ⓑ strong.
    - ● moist.

STOP

Benchmark 5

Benchmark 5

Grammar, Usage, and Mechanics

Read each question. Fill in the bubble beside the answer in each group that is correct. If none of the answers is correct, choose the last answer, "none of the above."

1. Which sentence is written correctly?
   - ● The Grand Canyon is in Arizona.
   - Ⓑ The grand Canyon is in Arizona.
   - Ⓒ The grand canyon is in Arizona.
   - Ⓓ none of the above

2. Which sentence is written correctly?
   - Ⓐ Aaron, Justine, Maria and Karen: are going to the movies today.
   - Ⓑ Aaron and Justine: Maria, Karen are going to the movies today.
   - Ⓒ Aaron: Justine, Maria and Karen are going to the movies today.
   - ● none of the above

3. Which sentence is written <u>incorrectly</u>?
   - Ⓐ We saw a play called <u>Easy Come, Easy Go</u>.
   - Ⓑ "The Raven" is my favorite poem.
   - ● A movie has been made out of the play "The Seagull."
   - Ⓓ none of the above

4. Which sentence is written correctly?
   - Ⓐ "Jose said, It isn't my turn yet."
   - Ⓑ Jose said, "It isn't my turn yet.
   - Ⓒ Jose said, It isn't my turn yet?
   - ● none of the above

5. Which sentence is written correctly?
   - ● The black dog is bigger than the white one.
   - Ⓑ The black dog is more bigger than the white one.
   - Ⓒ The black dog is most big than the white one.
   - Ⓓ none of the above

Benchmark 5

Benchmark 5

Grammar, Usage, and Mechanics (continued)

6. Which sentence is written correctly?
   - ● Luna and her brother go to the new elementary school.
   - Ⓑ Luna and her brother goes to the new elementary school.
   - Ⓒ Luna and her brother was going to the new elementary school.
   - Ⓓ none of the above

7. Which sentence is written <u>incorrectly</u>?
   - Ⓐ The grapes were too sour when I ate them.
   - Ⓑ I wore those gloves last winter.
   - ● Them is my favorite kinds of soup.
   - Ⓓ none of the above

8. Which sentence is written correctly?
   - Ⓐ The movie started after the previews are shown.
   - Ⓑ The movie starts after the previews were shown.
   - ● The movie started after the previews were shown.
   - Ⓓ none of the above

9. Which sentence contains a compound predicate?
   - ● The tide rose and flooded the marsh.
   - Ⓑ Look at the size of the apples on that tree.
   - Ⓒ The zoo parking lot was completely full.
   - Ⓓ none of the above

10. Which sentence contains a dependent clause?
    - ● You can go if you bring your sister.
    - Ⓑ My sister has a dog and a cat.
    - Ⓒ The photographer took a picture of the trees.
    - Ⓓ none of the above

STOP

Benchmark 5

Benchmark 5 Answer Sheets

Spelling

Read each group of words. Only one of the words is spelled correctly. Fill in the bubble under the word that is spelled correctly.

1. slippers   slipers   sllipers   slippirs
   ● Ⓐ   Ⓑ   Ⓒ   Ⓓ

2. giulty   guilty   guitly   giultey
   Ⓐ   ●   Ⓒ   Ⓓ

3. blod   bloode   bloud   blood
   Ⓐ   Ⓑ   Ⓒ   ●

4. paerl   pealr   pearl   peral
   Ⓐ   Ⓑ   ●   Ⓓ

5. stiars   stairs   staars   steirs
   Ⓐ   ●   Ⓒ   Ⓓ

GO ON →

Benchmark 5

Spelling (continued)

In each sentence, look for the underlined word that is spelled incorrectly. Focus on just the underlined word. Fill in the bubble next to the sentence with the misspelled word. If all the underlined words are spelled correctly, choose "correct as is."

6. Ⓐ Be sure to read the next <u>chapter</u>.
   Ⓑ Building a house takes a lot of <u>labor</u>.
   Ⓒ The wood felt <u>smooth</u> and hard.
   ● correct as is

7. Ⓐ The butcher must <u>sharpen</u> his knife.
   Ⓑ Aunt Julie wants tea with <u>lemon</u>.
   ● Dad gave us <u>permision</u> to go.
   Ⓓ correct as is

8. Ⓐ Work hard and you will <u>succeed</u>.
   Ⓑ The park is in a <u>central</u> place.
   Ⓒ <u>Load</u> up the truck and let's go.
   ● correct as is

9. Ⓐ The football player wore a <u>helmet</u>.
   ● Those coins are <u>valauble</u>.
   Ⓒ Make a <u>chart</u> for the classroom.
   Ⓓ correct as is

10. ● There are <u>thrity</u> houses on this block.
    Ⓑ The old bridge is <u>unsafe</u>.
    Ⓒ The fire burned down to <u>ashes</u>.
    Ⓓ correct as is

STOP This is the end of the group-administered section of the Benchmark Assessment.

Benchmark 5

Benchmark 6 Answer Sheets

Benchmark 6

Comprehension (continued)

1. This story is mostly about
   - Ⓐ how to improve a closet.
   - Ⓑ giving old clothes to charity.
   - Ⓒ a girl learning to organize.
   - Ⓓ the importance of being on time.

2. At the beginning of the story, Lynn can be described as
   - Ⓐ responsible.
   - Ⓑ clever.
   - Ⓒ disorganized.
   - Ⓓ healthy.

3. Why was Lynn late when the story begins?
   - Ⓐ She could not find her gym shoes.
   - Ⓑ Her dad could not find the car keys.
   - Ⓒ She was still doing her homework.
   - Ⓓ The school bus was stuck in traffic.

4. Why is Lynn's dad frowning at the beginning of the story?
   - Ⓐ He cannot find his keys.
   - Ⓑ He sees Lynn running late.
   - Ⓒ He knows that traffic is bad.
   - Ⓓ He is not happy about his job.

5. What will happen to Lynn if she is late again?
   - Ⓐ She will get detention.
   - Ⓑ She will have extra assignments.
   - Ⓒ Her dad will not be able to drive her.
   - Ⓓ Her backpack will be lost.

GO ON

86 • Level 4   Benchmark Assessment • Benchmark 6

Benchmark 6

Benchmark 6

Comprehension (continued)

6. Which of these did Lynn and her dad do first?
   - Ⓐ They sorted through her desk drawers.
   - Ⓑ They gave Lynn's old clothes to charity.
   - Ⓒ They threw out old papers.
   - Ⓓ They went through things under the bed.

7. It appears as if Lynn used her desk drawer as a
   - Ⓐ book shelf.
   - Ⓑ trash can.
   - Ⓒ sock drawer.
   - Ⓓ chalk box.

8. What does Lynn's dad say is the trick about organizing?
   - Ⓐ deciding what to throw out
   - Ⓑ deciding what to give away
   - Ⓒ keeping things where they belong
   - Ⓓ having enough boxes that are big

9. Why does Lynn think she will be on time tomorrow?
   - Ⓐ She will set her alarm correctly.
   - Ⓑ She will fix lunch the night before.
   - Ⓒ She will have a smaller breakfast.
   - Ⓓ She will be able to find things.

10. From this story, we know that Lynn's dad
    - Ⓐ is an organized person.
    - Ⓑ does not know the principal.
    - Ⓒ has an important job.
    - Ⓓ will not help her any more.

GO ON

Benchmark Assessment • Benchmark 6   Level 4 • 87

Benchmark 6

Benchmark 6

Comprehension (continued)

1. This selection is mostly about
   - Ⓐ scientists who study quicksand.
   - Ⓑ how dangerous quicksand is.
   - Ⓒ what quicksand is made of.
   - Ⓓ how quicksand really works.

2. Which of these describes quicksand most accurately?
   - Ⓐ It may be good for the health of some people.
   - Ⓑ It actually tickles when you get stuck.
   - Ⓒ It is not as dangerous as people think.
   - Ⓓ It is rarely more than two feet deep.

3. Which of these is not an ingredient of quicksand?
   - Ⓐ oxygen
   - Ⓑ fine sand
   - Ⓒ salt water
   - Ⓓ clay

4. What happens to quicksand over time?
   - Ⓐ It gets thinner.
   - Ⓑ It gets thicker.
   - Ⓒ It gets lighter.
   - Ⓓ It gets darker.

5. Why is quicksand dangerous?
   - Ⓐ It is very easy to drown in it.
   - Ⓑ It has ingredients that are poisonous.
   - Ⓒ It can cause diseases.
   - Ⓓ It is hard to get out of.

GO ON

90 • Level 4   Benchmark Assessment • Benchmark 6

Benchmark 6

Benchmark 6

Comprehension (continued)

6. A person in quicksand will sink about as deep as the person's
   - Ⓐ knee.
   - Ⓑ hip.
   - Ⓒ chest.
   - Ⓓ head.

7. It is hard to move in quicksand because it
   - Ⓐ hardens quickly once you fall in.
   - Ⓑ is extremely slippery.
   - Ⓒ gets denser once you fall in.
   - Ⓓ is less dense than your body.

8. What is something you should do if you fall in quicksand?
   - Ⓐ Do not move at all.
   - Ⓑ Get somebody to pull on your arms.
   - Ⓒ Thrash your arms and legs around.
   - Ⓓ Wiggle your legs a little bit.

9. Why should you not pull somebody out of quicksand quickly?
   - Ⓐ It might hurt them.
   - Ⓑ You will fall in, too.
   - Ⓒ Quicksand works too fast.
   - Ⓓ They would not survive.

10. From this selection, you know that
    - Ⓐ it is not possible to get out of quicksand.
    - Ⓑ falling in quicksand probably will not kill you.
    - Ⓒ quicksand does not smell very good.
    - Ⓓ most quicksand is found in the desert.

STOP

Benchmark Assessment • Benchmark 6   Level 4 • 91

Benchmark 6

Benchmark 6 Answer Sheets

Vocabulary

Read each item. Fill in the bubble for the answer you think is correct.

1. Athletic means
- Ⓐ almost finished.
- Ⓑ ready to leave.
- Ⓒ easily tired.
- ● good at sports.

2. Skill is the base word in skillful. Skillful means
- Ⓐ moving away from.
- ● having a special ability.
- Ⓒ without problems.
- Ⓓ not on time.

3. Autograph means
- ● a person's written name.
- Ⓑ prison.
- Ⓒ a place that is far away.
- Ⓓ thumb.

4. What word means about the same as popular?
- Ⓐ expensive
- ● liked
- Ⓒ crowded
- Ⓓ distant

5. What word means about the same as crisp?
- ● brisk
- Ⓑ warm
- Ⓒ muggy
- Ⓓ soggy

GO ON

Benchmark 6

Vocabulary (continued)

6. What word means the opposite of grinned?
- ● frowned
- Ⓒ smiled
- Ⓑ joined
- Ⓓ understood

7. Which word BEST completes both sentences?
Flour is made from ____.
This wood has a beautiful ____.
- ● grain
- Ⓒ finish
- Ⓑ wheat
- Ⓓ color

8. Which word BEST completes both sentences?
The park ____ needed paint.
The coach will ____ me if I am late.
- ● bench
- Ⓒ table
- Ⓑ lamp
- Ⓓ fire

9. The fearless knight never ran away.
Fearless means
- ● brave.
- Ⓒ smart.
- Ⓑ foolish.
- Ⓓ strong.

10. We all went to the wooden lodge to get warm.
Lodge means
- Ⓐ tent.
- Ⓒ diner.
- ● cabin.
- Ⓓ truck.

STOP

Benchmark 6

Grammar, Usage, and Mechanics

Read each question. Fill in the bubble beside the answer in each group that is correct. If none of the answers is correct, choose the last answer, "none of the above."

1. Which sentence is written correctly?
- Ⓐ The Doctor specializes in heart surgery.
- Ⓑ The doctor specializes in Heart Surgery.
- Ⓒ The Doctor specializes in Heart Surgery.
- ● none of the above

2. Which sentence is written correctly?
- ● Three families live near ours: the Smiths, the Johnsons, and the Ramones.
- Ⓑ Three families live near ours: The Smiths, the Johnsons, and the Ramones.
- Ⓒ Three families live near ours the Smiths, the Johnsons, and the Ramones.
- Ⓓ none of the above

3. Which sentence is written correctly?
- Ⓐ Many people have read E.B. White's novel, "Charlotte's Web."
- Ⓑ Many people have read E.B. White's novel, Charlotte's Web.
- ● Many people have read E.B. White's novel, Charlotte's Web.
- Ⓓ none of the above

4. Which sentence is written incorrectly?
- ● Clark said "Let's go into the cave."
- Ⓑ "It is too dark," said Milo.
- Ⓒ Clark replied, "Don't be so scared."
- Ⓓ none of the above

5. Which sentence is written correctly?
- Ⓐ Their car went into the last turn too fastly.
- Ⓑ Their car went into the last turn too faster.
- ● Their car went into the last turn too fast.
- Ⓓ none of the above

GO ON

Benchmark 6

Grammar, Usage, and Mechanics (continued)

6. Which sentence is written incorrectly?
- Ⓐ Dena and Will are helping their mother.
- Ⓑ When dad called, Greg and Gary came running.
- Ⓒ Justin and Aaron are raking the leaves.
- ● none of the above

7. Which sentence is written correctly?
- Ⓐ Them crackers taste funny.
- ● These crackers taste funny.
- Ⓒ They crackers taste funny.
- Ⓓ none of the above

8. Which sentence is written incorrectly?
- ● Grandmother will call me when she needed a ride.
- Ⓑ When I went to school, I rode a bus.
- Ⓒ One time, the bus nearly hit me when it passed.
- Ⓓ none of the above

9. Which sentence contains a compound predicate?
- Ⓐ The restaurant opens at six o'clock in the morning.
- ● Horses ran around the field or nibbled the grass.
- Ⓒ The meeting will take place in the auditorium.
- Ⓓ none of the above

10. Which sentence contains a dependent clause?
- Ⓐ Mr. Nichols had to shovel snow several times last winter.
- ● My mother likes the park when the pond is frozen.
- Ⓒ The hardware store is just down the street.
- Ⓓ none of the above

STOP

Benchmark 6

Benchmark 6 Answer Sheets

Spelling

Read each group of words. Only one of the words is spelled correctly. Fill in the bubble under the word that is spelled correctly.

1. flod   fleod   floode   **flood**
   Ⓐ   Ⓑ   ©   ●

2. sall   sela   **sale**   saile
   Ⓐ   Ⓑ   ●   Ⓓ

3. **limbs**   lims   libms   lmibs
   ●   Ⓑ   ©   Ⓓ

4. kicted   **kicked**   kikked   kickid
   Ⓐ   ●   ©   Ⓓ

5. pirde   prode   preide   **pride**
   Ⓐ   Ⓑ   ©   ●

GO ON →

Benchmark 6

Spelling (continued)

In each sentence, look for the underlined word that is spelled incorrectly. Focus on just the underlined word. Fill in the bubble next to the sentence with the misspelled word. If all the underlined words are spelled correctly, choose "correct as is."

6. Ⓐ The apple <u>blossoms</u> are out already.
   Ⓑ It <u>snowed</u> for three days in a row.
   ● Rain washed the <u>topsiol</u> away.
   Ⓓ correct as is

7. Ⓐ Fall <u>evenings</u> are chilly.
   Ⓑ There is too much <u>spice</u> in this soup.
   © Put your <u>napkin</u> in your lap.
   ● correct as is

8. Ⓐ Let's <u>continue</u> this tomorrow.
   ● The <u>athalete</u> played three sports.
   © Those socks are really <u>dirty</u>.
   Ⓓ correct as is

9. ● There was a <u>shortige</u> of food during the war.
   Ⓑ Close the <u>gate</u> when you leave.
   © <u>Traffic</u> was backed up on Main Street.
   Ⓓ correct as is

10. Ⓐ The sailor told us a strange <u>tale</u>.
    ● Dad is the store <u>manageer</u> here.
    © That movie was <u>shown</u> last week.
    Ⓓ correct as is

🛑 **STOP** This is the end of the group-administered section of the Benchmark Assessment.

Benchmark 6

Benchmark 7 Answer Sheets

Comprehension (continued)

1. This story is mostly about
   Ⓐ how to hit a baseball.
   Ⓑ how to choose a baseball team.
   Ⓒ how family support helps a boy.
   Ⓓ how much fun baseball is to play.

2. Which of these happens first?
   Ⓐ Juan helps Brad with batting practice.
   Ⓑ Juan's mother gives him a hug.
   Ⓒ Juan was a starting player on the team.
   Ⓓ Juan tries out for the baseball team.

3. Which of these is true about Juan's mother?
   Ⓐ She was the first female baseball player at her college.
   Ⓑ She does not really like baseball all that much.
   Ⓒ She played softball in high school and college.
   Ⓓ She is one of the coaches on Juan's team.

4. Why does Juan have a problem?
   Ⓐ He is afraid of getting hit with a baseball.
   Ⓑ He does not know the rules of the game.
   Ⓒ He does not have a glove and bat to use.
   Ⓓ He is not very good at playing baseball.

5. Why is Juan's mother proud?
   Ⓐ Her sons are all great players.
   Ⓑ Juan has tried his best.
   Ⓒ Brad hit a home run.
   Ⓓ She threw the ball the farthest.

GO ON →

Benchmark 7

Comprehension (continued)

6. You can conclude that Juan's brothers are
   Ⓐ good in school.
   Ⓑ older than Juan.
   Ⓒ good at other sports.
   Ⓓ hoping he joins their team.

7. How does Jerry help Juan?
   Ⓐ He tells the coach to make Juan a starter.
   Ⓑ He cheers for him during his first game.
   Ⓒ He shows him how to catch and throw.
   Ⓓ He teaches him to figure out how fast a pitch is.

8. How quickly does Juan improve at baseball?
   Ⓐ little by little
   Ⓑ right away
   Ⓒ over the course of years
   Ⓓ during the game

9. Why does Juan's family help him so much?
   Ⓐ They want him to be a star player.
   Ⓑ They want his team to win more.
   Ⓒ They want him to enjoy baseball.
   Ⓓ They want to start their own team.

10. From this story, you learn that
    Ⓐ even good players have to practice.
    Ⓑ Juan's parents met at a ball game.
    Ⓒ Brad is a better player than Jerry.
    Ⓓ the coach picked Juan last.

GO ON →

Benchmark 7

Comprehension (continued)

1. This selection is mostly about
   Ⓐ how Father's Day came to be.
   Ⓑ the very first Father's Day card.
   Ⓒ Father's Day in other countries.
   Ⓓ what Father's Day means to people.

2. The first Father's Day card was unusual because it
   Ⓐ had a picture of an animal.
   Ⓑ was given to a president.
   Ⓒ told a funny story.
   Ⓓ was made of clay.

3. How do we know about the first Father's Day card?
   Ⓐ The card was written in English.
   Ⓑ The card, a clay tablet, still exists.
   Ⓒ The ancestors of the boy who sent the card retell his story.
   Ⓓ The father of the boy who sent the card was a famous man.

4. From this selection, you know that
   Ⓐ holidays are the same around the world.
   Ⓑ people did not think we needed Father's Day.
   Ⓒ fathers have been thanked through the years.
   Ⓓ Father's Day began in Europe.

5. Sonora Smart Dodd got her idea for Father's Day from
   Ⓐ a talk about how important mothers are.
   Ⓑ her five brothers and sisters.
   Ⓒ not knowing when her father's birthday was.
   Ⓓ reading about a young boy from Babylon.

GO ON →

Benchmark 7

Comprehension (continued)

6. Which of these is true about Sonora Smart Dodd's mother?
   Ⓐ She raised six children by herself.
   Ⓑ She died when Dodd was young.
   Ⓒ She helped Dodd start Father's Day.
   Ⓓ She lived in Washington long ago.

7. Where did Sonora Smart Dodd live when she started Father's Day?
   Ⓐ North Carolina
   Ⓑ New York
   Ⓒ Florida
   Ⓓ Washington

8. Who made Father's Day a national holiday?
   Ⓐ Sonora Smart Dodd
   Ⓑ Jobe
   Ⓒ Ms. Dodd's father
   Ⓓ Congress

9. When was Father's Day first celebrated in the United States?
   Ⓐ 1972
   Ⓑ 1910
   Ⓒ 2000
   Ⓓ 1776

10. From the selection you learn that Father's Day
    Ⓐ began as a holiday for fathers and mothers.
    Ⓑ is always on the first Sunday in June.
    Ⓒ took a while to establish as a holiday.
    Ⓓ is only celebrated in a few countries.

STOP

Benchmark 7

Benchmark 7 Answer Sheets

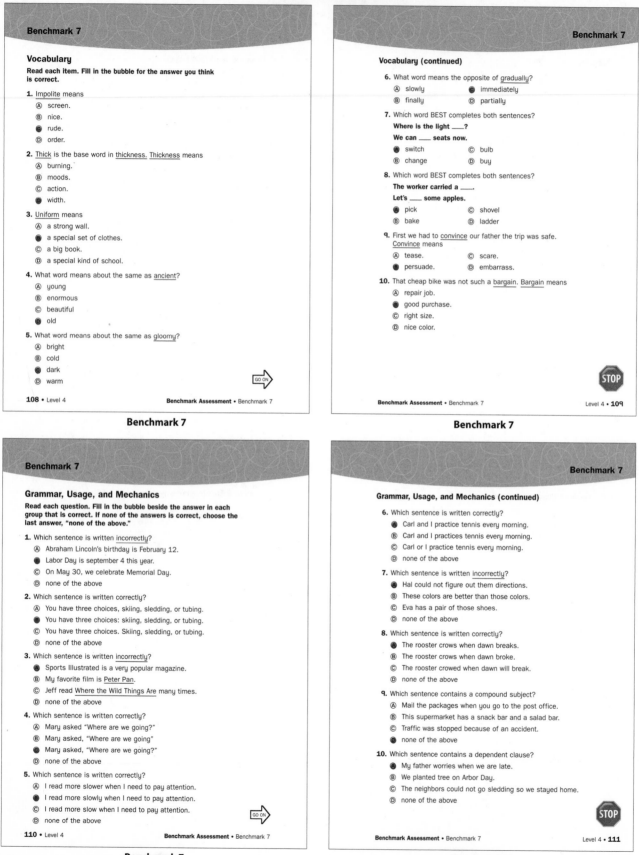

Benchmark 7

Vocabulary

Read each item. Fill in the bubble for the answer you think is correct.

1. Impolite means
   - Ⓐ screen.
   - Ⓑ nice.
   - ● rude.
   - Ⓓ order.

2. Thick is the base word in thickness. Thickness means
   - Ⓐ burning.
   - Ⓑ moods.
   - Ⓒ action.
   - ● width.

3. Uniform means
   - Ⓐ a strong wall.
   - ● a special set of clothes.
   - Ⓒ a big book.
   - Ⓓ a special kind of school.

4. What word means about the same as ancient?
   - Ⓐ young
   - Ⓑ enormous
   - Ⓒ beautiful
   - ● old

5. What word means about the same as gloomy?
   - Ⓐ bright
   - Ⓑ cold
   - ● dark
   - Ⓓ warm

Benchmark Assessment • Benchmark 7

Benchmark 7

Vocabulary (continued)

6. What word means the opposite of gradually?
   - Ⓐ slowly
   - ● immediately
   - Ⓑ finally
   - Ⓓ partially

7. Which word BEST completes both sentences?
   Where is the light ____?
   We can ____ seats now.
   - ● switch
   - Ⓒ bulb
   - Ⓑ change
   - Ⓓ buy

8. Which word BEST completes both sentences?
   The worker carried a ____.
   Let's ____ some apples.
   - ● pick
   - Ⓒ shovel
   - Ⓑ bake
   - Ⓓ ladder

9. First we had to convince our father the trip was safe. Convince means
   - Ⓐ tease.
   - Ⓒ scare.
   - ● persuade.
   - Ⓓ embarrass.

10. That cheap bike was not such a bargain. Bargain means
    - Ⓐ repair job.
    - ● good purchase.
    - Ⓒ right size.
    - Ⓓ nice color.

STOP

Benchmark Assessment • Benchmark 7

Benchmark 7

Benchmark 7

Grammar, Usage, and Mechanics

Read each question. Fill in the bubble beside the answer in each group that is correct. If none of the answers is correct, choose the last answer, "none of the above."

1. Which sentence is written incorrectly?
   - Ⓐ Abraham Lincoln's birthday is February 12.
   - ● Labor Day is september 4 this year.
   - Ⓒ On May 30, we celebrate Memorial Day.
   - Ⓓ none of the above

2. Which sentence is written correctly?
   - Ⓐ You have three choices, skiing, sledding, or tubing.
   - ● You have three choices: skiing, sledding, or tubing.
   - Ⓒ You have three choices. Skiing, sledding, or tubing.
   - Ⓓ none of the above

3. Which sentence is written incorrectly?
   - ● Sports Illustrated is a very popular magazine.
   - Ⓑ My favorite film is Peter Pan.
   - Ⓒ Jeff read Where the Wild Things Are many times.
   - Ⓓ none of the above

4. Which sentence is written correctly?
   - Ⓐ Mary asked "Where are we going?"
   - Ⓑ Mary asked, "Where are we going"
   - ● Mary asked, "Where are we going?"
   - Ⓓ none of the above

5. Which sentence is written correctly?
   - Ⓐ I read more slower when I need to pay attention.
   - ● I read more slowly when I need to pay attention.
   - Ⓒ I read more slow when I need to pay attention.
   - Ⓓ none of the above

Benchmark Assessment • Benchmark 7

Benchmark 7

Grammar, Usage, and Mechanics (continued)

6. Which sentence is written correctly?
   - ● Carl and I practice tennis every morning.
   - Ⓑ Carl and I practices tennis every morning.
   - Ⓒ Carl or I practice tennis every morning.
   - Ⓓ none of the above

7. Which sentence is written incorrectly?
   - ● Hal could not figure out them directions.
   - Ⓑ These colors are better than those colors.
   - Ⓒ Eva has a pair of those shoes.
   - Ⓓ none of the above

8. Which sentence is written correctly?
   - ● The rooster crows when dawn breaks.
   - Ⓑ The rooster crows when dawn broke.
   - Ⓒ The rooster crowed when dawn will break.
   - Ⓓ none of the above

9. Which sentence contains a compound subject?
   - Ⓐ Mail the packages when you go to the post office.
   - Ⓑ This supermarket has a snack bar and a salad bar.
   - Ⓒ Traffic was stopped because of an accident.
   - ● none of the above

10. Which sentence contains a dependent clause?
    - ● My father worries when we are late.
    - Ⓑ We planted tree on Arbor Day.
    - Ⓒ The neighbors could not go sledding so we stayed home.
    - Ⓓ none of the above

STOP

Benchmark Assessment • Benchmark 7

Benchmark 7

Benchmark 7

Spelling

Read each group of words. Only one of the words is spelled correctly. Fill in the bubble under the word that is spelled correctly.

1. firend   friend   freind   friedn
    Ⓐ   ●   Ⓒ   Ⓓ

2. arena   arnea   aerena   erana
    ●   Ⓑ   Ⓒ   Ⓓ

3. expresed   expresst   expressed   acspresed
    Ⓐ   Ⓑ   ●   Ⓓ

4. gaurdian   guardian   guardain   guadrian
    Ⓐ   ●   Ⓒ   Ⓓ

5. mammels   mammils   mamals   mammals
    Ⓐ   Ⓑ   Ⓒ   ●

GO ON →

Benchmark 7

Benchmark 7

Spelling (continued)

In each sentence, look for the underlined word that is spelled incorrectly. Focus on just the underlined word. Fill in the bubble next to the sentence with the misspelled word. If all the underlined words are spelled correctly, choose "correct as is."

6. Ⓐ Brenda <u>blushes</u> easily.
   ● This change is <u>permenant</u>.
   Ⓒ Casey <u>challenged</u> his friend.
   Ⓓ correct as is

7. Ⓐ The truck needed a new <u>moter</u>.
   Ⓑ My brother likes to <u>wrestle</u> with me.
   Ⓒ All the guards were on <u>alert</u>.
   Ⓓ correct as is

8. Ⓐ Can you <u>operate</u> that machine?
   Ⓑ Steve's <u>handwriting</u> is beautiful.
   Ⓒ That <u>area</u> is closed.
   ● correct as is

9. Ⓐ Patsy is a <u>lively</u> person.
   ● The captain was <u>giuding</u> the ship.
   Ⓒ The police <u>caught</u> the robber.
   Ⓓ correct as is

10. Ⓐ Isn't this weather just <u>dreadful</u>?
    Ⓑ Reading <u>ghost</u> stories is a lot of fun.
    ● Waiting for Ben after school takes <u>pateince</u>.
    Ⓓ correct as is

STOP This is the end of the group-administered section of the Benchmark Assessment.

Benchmark 7

Four Point Rubrics for Expository Writing

Genre	1 Point	2 Points	3 Points	4 Points
Expository	Composition has no introduction or clear topic. It offers a group of loosely related facts or a series of poorly written steps. No conclusion is included.	Composition is clearly organized around main points with supportive facts or assertions. Composition has no clear introduction, but its topic is identifiable. However, it includes many facts unrelated to the topic, or it describes things in a disorganized way. No conclusion is included.	Main points and supportive details can be identified, but they are not clearly marked. Composition has an introduction and offers facts about the topic. Some facts may be irrelevant, or some ideas may be vague or out of order. The report is fairly well organized but doesn't have a strong conclusion.	Traces and constructs a line of argument, identifying part-to-whole relations. Main points are supported with logical and appropriate evidence. Composition begins with an introduction and offers relevant facts about the topic or describes the topic appropriately. The report is organized using cause/effect, comparison/contrast, or another pattern. It ends with a strong conclusion

Writing Traits

	1 Point	2 Points	3 Points	4 Points
Focus	Topic is unclear or wanders and must be inferred. Extraneous material may be present.	Topic/position/direction is unclear and must be inferred.	Topic/position is stated and direction/purpose is previewed and maintained. Mainly stays on topic.	Topic/position is clearly stated, previewed, and maintained throughout the paper. Topics and details are tied together with a central theme or purpose that is maintained/threaded throughout the paper.
Ideas/Content	Superficial and/or minimal content is included.	Main ideas are understandable, although they may be overly broad or simplistic, and the results may not be effective. Supporting detail is limited, insubstantial, overly general or off topic.	The writing is clear and focused. The reader can easily understand the main ideas. Support is present, although it may be limited or rather general.	Writing is exceptionally clear, focused, and interesting. Main ideas stand out and are developed by strong support and rich details.
Elaboration (supporting details and examples that develop the main idea)	States ideas or points with minimal detail to support them.	Includes sketchy, redundant, or general details; some may be irrelevant. Support for key ideas is very uneven.	Includes mix of general statements and specific details/examples. Support is mostly relevant but may be uneven and lack depth in places.	Includes specific details and supporting examples for each key point/idea. May use compare/contrast to support.

Writing Conventions

	1 Point	2 Points	3 Points	4 Points
Conventions Overall	Numerous errors in usage, grammar, spelling, capitalization, and punctuation repeatedly distract the reader and make the text difficult to read. The reader finds it difficult to focus on the message.	The writing demonstrates limited control of standard writing conventions (punctuation, spelling, capitalization, grammar, and usage). Errors sometimes impede readability.	The writing demonstrates control of standard writing conventions (punctuation, spelling, capitalization, grammar, and usage). Minor errors, while perhaps noticeable, do not impede readability.	The writing demonstrates exceptionally strong control of standard writing conventions (punctuation, spelling, capitalization, grammar, and usage) and uses them effectively to enhance communication. Errors are so few and so minor that the reader can easily skim over them.

Benchmark Assessment Record

Student Name	Comprehension (40 points)	Vocabulary (30 points)	Grammar, Usage, and Mechanics (20 points)	Spelling (10 points)	Total Score	Cutoff Reached? (20 points)	Fluency (WPM)	Cutoff Reached? (68 words)	Writing Prompt Cutoff Reached?

Benchmark Assessment 2

Benchmark Assessment Record

Student Name	Comprehension (40 points)	Vocabulary (30 points)	Grammar, Usage, and Mechanics (20 points)	Spelling (10 points)	Total Score	Cutoff Reached? (30 points)	Fluency (WPM)	Cutoff Reached? (82 words)

Benchmark Assessment Record

Student Name	Comprehension (40 points)	Vocabulary (30 points)	Grammar, Usage, and Mechanics (20 points)	Spelling (10 points)	Total Score	Cutoff Reached? (42 points)	Fluency (WPM)	Cutoff Reached? (96 words)

Benchmark Assessment 4

Benchmark Assessment Record

Student Name	Comprehension (40 points)	Vocabulary (30 points)	Grammar, Usage, and Mechanics (20 points)	Spelling (10 points)	Total Score	Cutoff Reached? (54 points)	Fluency (WPM)	Cutoff Reached? (110 words)	Writing Prompt Cutoff Reached?

Benchmark Assessment Record

Student Name	Comprehension (40 points)	Vocabulary (30 points)	Grammar, Usage, and Mechanics (20 points)	Spelling (10 points)	Total Score	Cutoff Reached? (66 points)	Fluency (WPM)	Cutoff Reached? (124 words)

Benchmark Assessment 6

Benchmark Assessment Record

Student Name	Comprehension (40 points)	Vocabulary (30 points)	Grammar, Usage, and Mechanics (20 points)	Spelling (10 points)	Total Score	Cutoff Reached? (78 points)	Fluency (WPM)	Cutoff Reached? (138 words)

Benchmark Assessment Record

Student Name	Comprehension (40 points)	Vocabulary (30 points)	Grammar, Usage, and Mechanics (20 points)	Spelling (10 points)	Total Score	Cutoff Reached? (90 points)	Fluency (WPM)	Cutoff Reached? (152 words)	Writing Prompt Cutoff Reached?

Benchmark Tracking Chart

Name _____

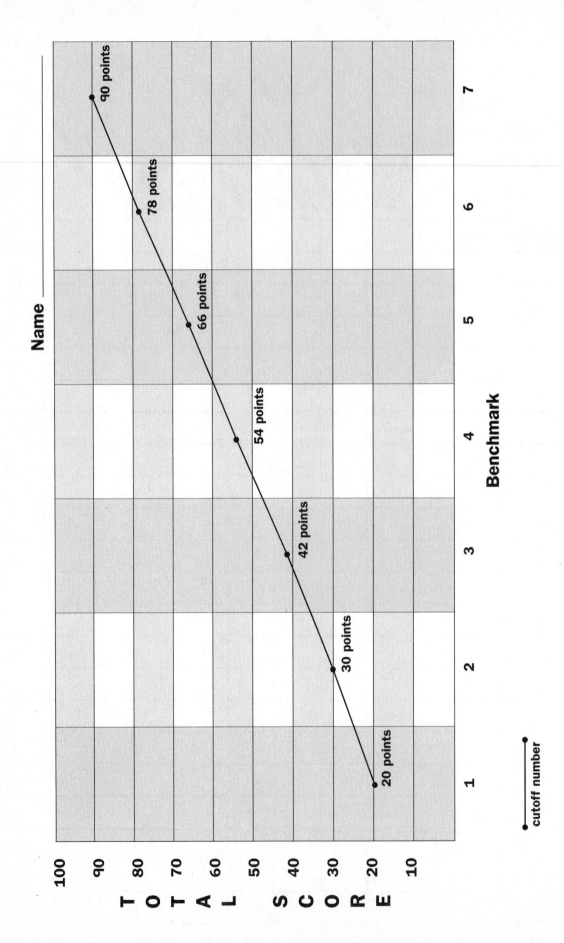

- 90 points
- 78 points
- 66 points
- 54 points
- 42 points
- 30 points
- 20 points

Benchmark: 1, 2, 3, 4, 5, 6, 7

TOTAL SCORE: 100, 90, 80, 70, 60, 50, 40, 30, 20, 10

cutoff number

Benchmark Assessment • Benchmark Tracking Chart